HOW TO
MAKE MONEY WITH A
DRONE

Discovering Your Niche, Finding Customers, and Getting Paid, In The Shortest, Most Cost-Effective Way Possible; Even If You've Never Flown A Drone.

New edition-updated for 2026.
By Mike Sobola

Copyright © 2023-2026 by Mike Sobola

All rights reserved. No part of this publication may be reproduced, stored or transmitted in any form or by any means, electronic, mechanical, photocopying, recording, scanning, or otherwise without written permission from the publisher. It is illegal to copy this book, post it to a website, or distribute it by any other means without permission.

Mike Sobola has no responsibility for the persistence or accuracy of URLs for external or third-party Internet Websites referred to in this publication and does not guarantee that any content on such websites is, or will remain, accurate or appropriate. Designations used by companies to distinguish their products are often claimed as trademarks. All brand names and product names used in this book and on its cover are trade names, service marks, trademarks and registered trademarks of their respective owners. The publishers and the book are not associated with any product or vendor mentioned in this book. None of the companies referenced within the book have endorsed the book.

While the publisher and author have used their best efforts in preparing this book, they make no representations or warranties with respect to the accuracy or completeness of the contents of this book and expressly disclaim any implied warranties of suitability for a particular purpose. No warranty may be created or extended by sales representatives or written sales materials. The advice and strategies contained herein may not be suitable for your situation, and you should consult with a professional when appropriate. Neither the publisher nor the author shall be liable for any loss of profit or any other commercial damages, including but not limited to special, incidental, consequential, personal, or other damages.

Second Edition-Updated January, 2026.

For Helen, my life partner who cheers on my wild ideas.

And for Ally, the light of our lives.

Contents

Introduction/What's New   VI

1. Licenses & Certifications   1

2. Getting Started   5

3. How Much Can I Make?   7

4. Startup Costs   11

5. Still Photography with Drones   23

6. Shooting Drone Video   29

7. Editing Your Video   35

8. Getting Experience & Getting Paid   37

9. Finding Clients   41

10. Emerging Industries for Drone Services   43

11. Established Drone Industries & How to Get the Work   61

12. Parting Words   83

13. 15-Day Action Plan   85

14. Your Free Gifts   93

References   95

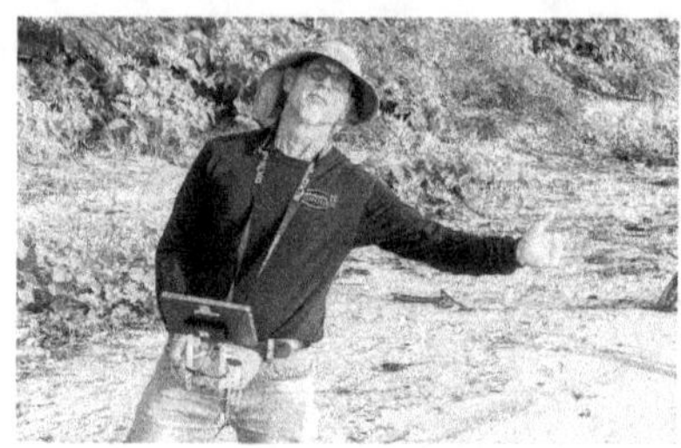

Introduction:
What's New in This Edition

"The only way to discover the limits of the possible
is to go beyond them into the impossible."

-Arthur C. Clarke

Additions to this Edition

For 2026, we've added or updated a number of areas to reflect the reality of flying drones commercially in today's rapidly-changing political and economic climate. This includes:

- New chapters on drone photography and cinematography plus best practices for editing done video;

- Opportunities in new and emerging drone industries such as crop spraying and seeding, renewable energy inspection, sewer, pipe & enclosed space inspection, and window & exterior facility washing via drone (a market that is projected to exceed US $2 billion by 2028);

- An updated list of drones for specific industries and jobs;

- And updates on laws and regulations affecting drones and drone operations.

Model Rockets and Flying Ships

I've always loved things that fly. I got my first model rocket when I was 10 by selling magazine subscriptions to my neighbors and my first drone in 2015. I can't think of a better way to make a living. If you're looking to start your own drone business, where do you begin? Questions like "How much can I make?", "What drone should I fly?", "Do I need a license?", and "How do I find clients?" make even the most gung-ho self-starter pause and reconsider. Plus, new laws, regulations and now, import restrictions have made things even more complicated.

Fortunately, in this book I've set out to answer all of these questions and more, as I explain:

- How to start your drone business quickly & efficiently;

- Finding the right drone at the right price for what you want to do;

- Shortcuts to making money right away-even while you learn;

- Where to find work, including who to contact & what they want;

- Ways to get real experience fast, and build your flying hours quickly;

- Pitfalls to avoid from a pilot who's been there.

Plus, there's an updated list of specific areas where drone opportunities are hottest, including how to find the work, what skills and equipment you need to start, and what you should charge for your missions. There's even a "15-Day Easy Action Plan" to help you start putting money in your pocket faster. Later, you'll find links to online instruction, shot examples, specific drone tips & techniques, and access to a FREE online FAA Part 107 preparation course (U.S.).

Laws and Regulations

Before we get started, it's important to note that, while most information is applicable to anywhere in the world, any laws and regulations mentioned here are clearly delineated as to where they apply-mainly the United States or the EU.

For other countries, please consult the local drone laws and licensing requirements applicable to where you will be flying. You can find information on drone laws by country, state or city by going to https://drone-laws.com. Click on the three lines in the upper left corner, scroll to your country, state or city and select it to see the laws in that region.

In this book, I'll mainly be discussing drones classified as "Small UAS" by the FAA in the United States-which is any drone under 55 lbs. This includes most hobby and professional drones that you'll more than likely be using in your business. And while I will be providing tips and further resources for effective flying techniques, camera settings, and how to get great shots, this is not an instruction manual on how to operate your drone. That information can all be found in the aircraft's technical manual that comes from the drone manufacturer itself.

A Word About Safety

As you get started in your new venture, keep in mind that you are flying an aircraft with the potential to cause harm to people, animals and other objects below and in your flight path. It's important to follow all manufacturer recommendations and your aviation authority airspace regulations at all times to help ensure safe operations and avoid injury. Now let's take off.

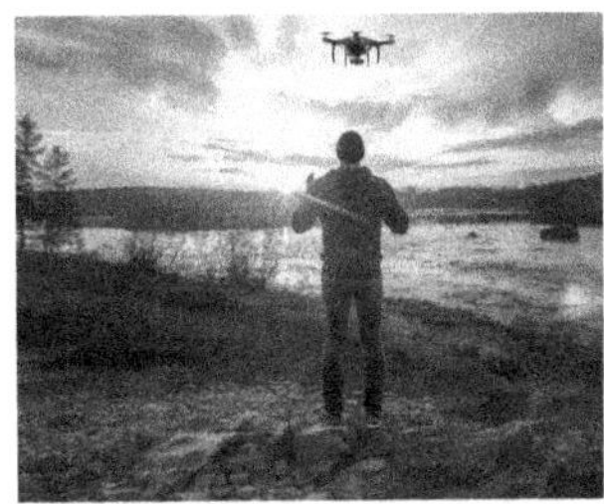

Chapter 1:
Licenses and Certifications

"Once you have tasted flight, you will forever walk the earth with your eyes turned skyward, for there you have been, and there you will always long to return."

-Leonardo Di Vinci

It's exciting when your drone license comes in the mail; your ticket to being paid for what you love to do. In the United States, it's officially known as a "Remote Pilot Certificate" and anytime you are benefiting from your flights (not just monetarily), you are considered a "Commercial Drone Pilot" and you'll need to have one. (I'll briefly cover EU requirements a bit later in this chapter.)

The U.S. Federal regulations that cover drone use are in "Part 107" of the Federal Regulations, so you may hear this referred to as the "Part 107 License", or "Drone License", but they are all talking about the same thing. Go to www.FAA.gov and click on "Drones" for specific information and procedures about getting your license.

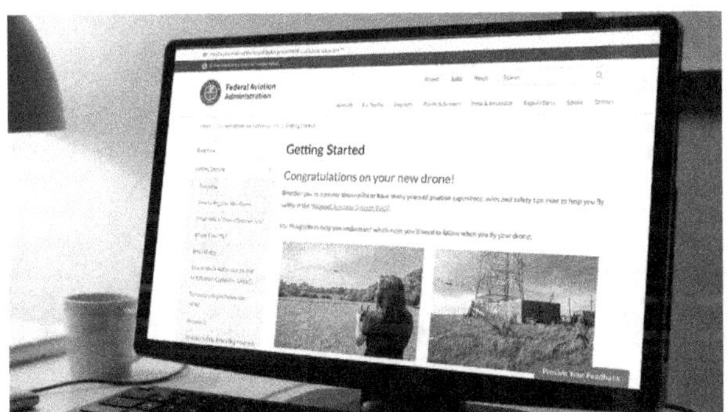

The FAA website is a good starting point in the U.S.

The FAA drone exam covers everything from airspace rules and regulations to aviation maps and weather forecasts. As of the publication of this book, there is no practical flying test, only the written exam. You can find study resources on the internet to help you prepare for the exam-including on the FAA website itself. Pick one that works for you. My company (Mid-Atlantic Drones) has put together a FREE Part 107 video study course that covers most everything you should know to pass the Part 107 Remote Pilot Exam, including sample test questions. You can access it through my website resource page by going to www.MikeSobola.com/resources. Here, you'll find links to the FREE study course as well as other links to information, regulations and a wide-range of other resources mentioned or alluded to throughout this book.

The exam itself must be taken at an FAA-Approved "Knowledge Testing Center" (you can find a list here: https://faa.psiexams.com.) It's a multiple-choice exam and the non-refundable cost (at the time this book was written) is $175.00. You'll have two hours to take it and must pass with a grade of at least 70% correct. If you don't pass, you'll have to wait 14 calendar days before you can re-take it. Once you get your license, you'll need to take a "recurrent" exam every 24 months to continue flying as a Commercial Drone Pilot. The recurrent exam is free and taken online through the FAA website. There is no practical hands-on flying test.

More Information

If you need more help, there are plenty of opportunities to pay for instruction if you prefer that route. Just make sure the company you choose is reputable, and ask for a guarantee. Some schools actually refund your course cost if you don't pass the exam on the first go-around, but most places simply let you take the course again for free.

Commercial Drone Flying in the EU

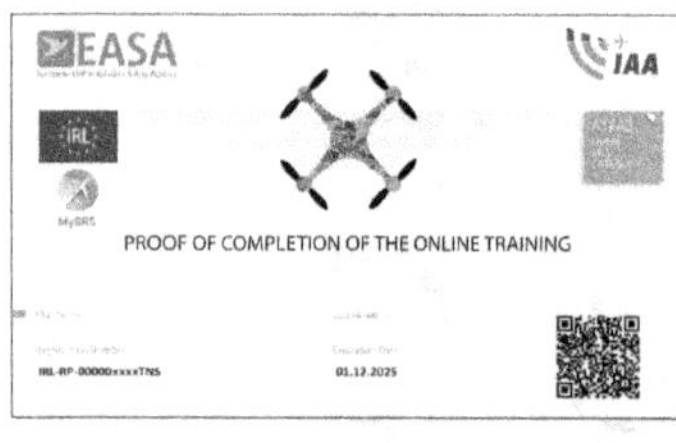

The drone consortium for the EU is the European Aviation Safety Authority, or EASA. It does not distinguish between recreational or commercial drone use, but _does_ look at drone weight, specifications, and your intended operation. To fly in the EU, you've got to register as an operator at your national aviation authority's website. Before you do that, you may want to find out the class of drone you have or intend on flying, as this will dictate where you can legally fly. There are a total of seven classes, from C0 to C6. When you register, your aviation authority will give you an **operator registration number** which must be attached to your aircraft. Use the same number for all of your drones. Then, take the drone test and get your certification. At that point, your certificate or license allow you to fly your drone in any EU member state.

If you're outside of the EU, you're supposed to take the test through the EU member state that you are first planning on flying in. But, you can actually take your drone test via <u>any</u> EU member's aviation authority. I recommend looking at Ireland, Luxembourg, Malta, or the Netherlands. These countries are known for easy online registration, English-language support, and fast processing times.

For links to all EU aviation authorities, go to: https://www.easa.europa.eu/en/domains/civil-drones/naa.

Anyone flying a drone in the EU is required to have an EASA drone license, but the type depends on the category you'll be flying under. Briefly, they've broken it up into 3 major categories: **Open, Specific, and Certified.** Certified is mainly for air transport taxis and drone deliveries, so you can probably forget about that one. Most recreational and low-risk commercial drone operations fall under the "Open" Category, and riskier operations not covered under "Open" will fall in the "Specific" category. In addition, the EU regulations require that the drone owner/operator registers themself *not the drone*. It also requires insurance if you're operating any drone over 25kg (and specific other cases depending on the member state). Certificates are valid for five years.

In the UK, regulations updated on January 1, 2026 require pilots to take a "Flyer ID Test" before they can fly a drone outside. For information on this visit this link: https://www.caa.co.uk/drones/getting-started-with-drones-and-model-aircraft/prepare-for-the-flyer-id-theory-test/.

Recreational Flying in the U.S.

If you're a pilot flying for fun in the U.S., the FAA says you still have to pass *The Recreational UAS Safety Test*, or "TRUST". This helps keep all of us safe by making sure everyone who flies a drone has at least thought about airspace rules and has some idea of what's right and what's wrong. The online test is free through one of the companies listed as test administrators on the FAA website. Once you pass, you'll get a certificate that you should have with you anytime you're flying. If you're a commercial operator, it's also a good idea to get the TRUST certificate so can fly under the less-restrictive recreational rules when you practice. See the "Resources" chapter for a link. In either case, recreational or commercial, the fun of flying starts after the certification. Get it, be safe, and start having fun.

Now let's go fly.

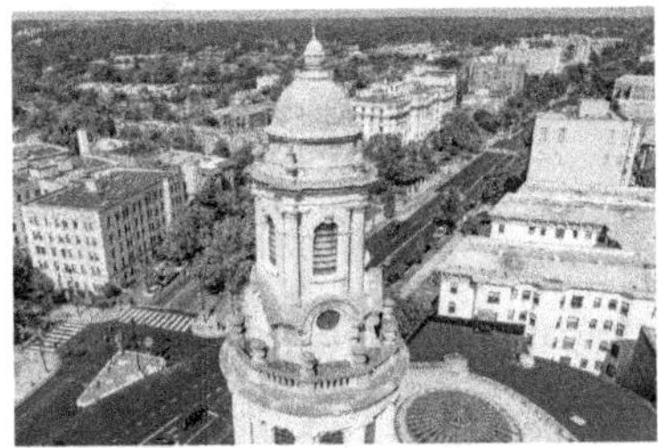

Chapter 2:
Getting Started

"The view from above is always worth the climb"
-Aime J. Kaufman

Congratulations, you're officially a licensed Drone Pilot. Now what? Before you go out, drop all your money on a drone and start looking for work, look at possible industries you might want to fly for. Cinematography for videos and movies? Construction data imaging? Crop spraying and plant health checks? Or maybe even...window washing? More importantly, think about your goal: full time, freelance, or part-time gig?

Slow and Steady

A slow approach might be good for you if you're not ready to leave your day job, or you don't have all the time and money to invest in your new business that you'd like to. With this strategy, you spend as little money as possible to get those first jobs, and at the same time re-invest everything into the business as you get paid. You'll still need your drone "license", the drone itself, and insurance, but your initial investment will be smaller than going full-time.

If drones can add value to your current job, try taking it a step further. Talk to your boss about how a drone department can help the business and volunteer to head up the "new department". Make sure you have the facts and figures to back it up. You'll probably still have your current responsibilities on top of the new tasks, so take that into consideration, as well.

Consider finding a mentor and immerse yourself in a practical training program so you can develop solid skills. Be creative when it comes to the approach you take and how you make it work in your unique situation. Starting small is less risky and minimizes initial outlay on equipment, marketing, and training-and that saves you money, but also results in extra work and a slow ramp-up to profitability.

Full Commitment

On the other hand, to go "all-in" , you'll have to turn your full attention to the new business, have both the time and financial resources to invest in it, and the desire to grow as fast as possible. Choosing to go big means you'll be setting your business up with the resources you need to quickly land jobs and get them done right. You'll need a pool of cash and a line of credit to pull from because, no matter how successful you project your plan to be, you won't have regular cash coming in until you really get established. You'll need skilled pilots and crew-either staff or freelance-to pick up any overlap.

This approach requires more than on-the-job self-teaching. You'll need a focused program of training using a mix of in-person and online resources. In both cases, you'll need a business plan, but going "all-in" requires an in-depth analysis of the industries you plan on serving, a realistic look at the potential revenue that serving those industries can bring your business and how you intend to get that business.

Both approaches require patience as you gain momentum and learn your craft. And whether your game plan is slow and sure or fast and furious, you'll still need to take certain steps to grow your business and assure success. It's up to you as to how much time and resources you want to allocate to do so. Your decision here will affect everything else down the line-including your time and availability, the amount of money you'll need to initially invest, and your profit margin. So, dive in, do your homework and come up with a plan. The next few chapters will help you do just that!

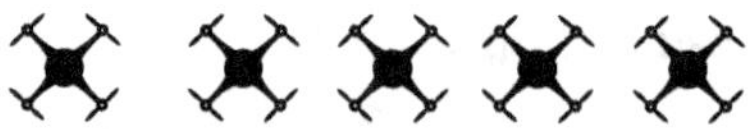

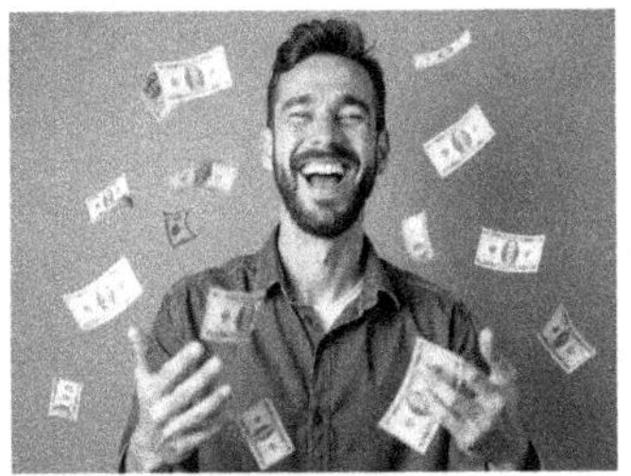

Chapter 3:
How Much Can I make?

"The higher we soar, the smaller we appear
to those who cannot fly."
-Fredrich Nietzsche

According to Glassdoor.com, the median pay for a full-time drone pilot in the United States in 2025 was $101,000.00 a year which works out to about $50 per hour for a 40-hour week. As a self-employed pilot, you can make more than three times that hourly rate, but you'll have to factor in all your time and expenses. Your specific rate will depend on the market you're in, what you're offering and what your customers want. Typically, a new freelance pilot can expect to make $20-$75 per hour, and experienced pilots, $75-$200 per hour.

Behind-The-Scenes

Keep in mind that you might need specialized equipment and that the job doesn't end when you land the aircraft. There's processing, editing, extracting data and uploading files. All of this takes time-and that's time you won't be spending on other projects. Other factors that have a direct influence on how much you'll make include:

- The type of drone and other equipment you own;

- Your relevant connections and background;

- Any drone and drone-related training you've taken;

- Where you're located and the industries you can target;

- And the amount of relative experience you have flying drones.

Turn the page to take a look at these areas and their impact on how much you can realistically expect to make flying your drone.

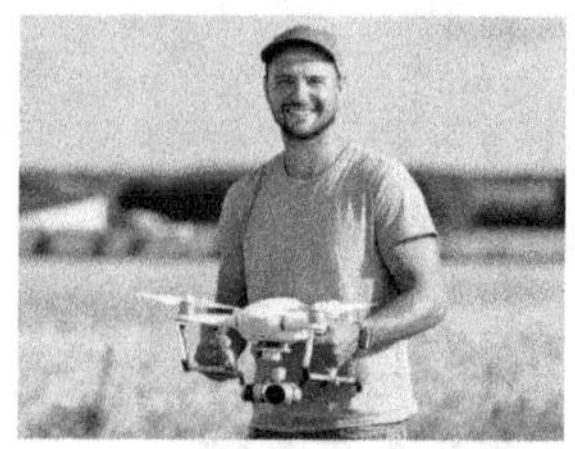

Your Experience

No matter what you do, the more experience you have, the better you'll be at your craft and the more you can generally charge. Plus, with more experience, you'll fly more efficiently and instinctually. And don't forget-as you get better and have more jobs, you're able to turn down lower-paying work in favor of the higher priced gigs. As a beginner you're being paid not only in money, but also in relevant experience that you can build on and use to become a better pilot and business owner. Sometimes, you may even be flying for free just to make the connection, get the experience, or to show the client what you can do for them.

In all these cases, you're adding to your arsenal of experience that you'll be able to pull from the rest of your piloting career. Be aware that some clients don't value experience and only want the lowest price. This is particularly true where AI and automation are involved. In those cases, you'll need to judge for yourself whether a particular job or client is worth taking.

The Type of Drone You Own

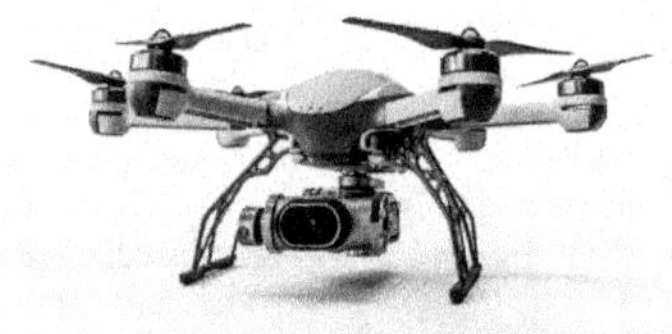

Bigger is not always better, but the difference between a drone with a fixed focal length camera, for instance, and a drone with interchangeable lenses, is huge. Sometimes clients will request certain lenses or camera capabilities that your fixed focal length lens does not have. In addition, larger and more complex drones mean you may be able to attach heavier cameras and fly the drone with a crew of two (Pilot and a Camera Operator) allowing for more flexibility, a better range of shot options, and a larger variety of potential clients. Manufacturers are trending towards more specialized drones, allowing them to carry out their intended tasks better. That means better imaging and data for the client, but a higher cost of entry for drone pilots who work across multiple industries.

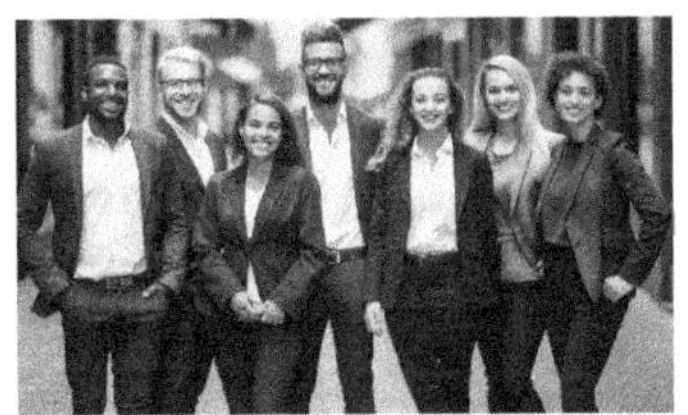

Your Connections

Your experience outside of flying drones can benefit your new career as a drone pilot. Think about what you're doing now or have done in the past-for pay or volunteer. That experience and those connections can be valuable when looking at industries to serve. If you're targeting the construction industry, for instance, and you have a background in that field or a related one, chances are you still have personal contacts that you can reach out to with your drone services.

Your background also gives you the "fluency" you need to successfully talk to those in the industry you're targeting which helps you to better understand their needs and how you can address them with your drone services. Don't be afraid to use that. Study current SOPs and question how drones might be able to streamline a process or capture better data than what's being done currently. That can translate into a recurring business and a dependable revenue stream.

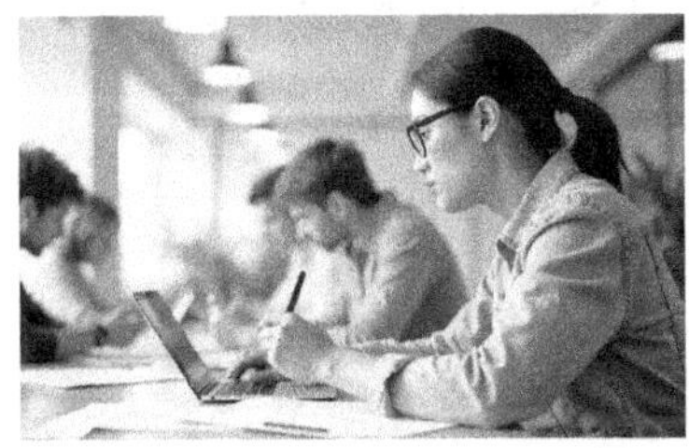

Your Training

If you don't necessarily have a background in the industry you want to target, don't rely on practice alone to get you there. Take a training course to fill in the gaps. Structured programs can teach you the exact terminology, safety standards, and workflow expectations professionals use in that field. Many drone pilots find that certified training shortens the learning curve and opens doors to higher-paying contracts. In some cases, specialized credentials or manufacturer training may even be required before you can operate commercially or bid on inspection projects. I'll go into this a bit later in the book.

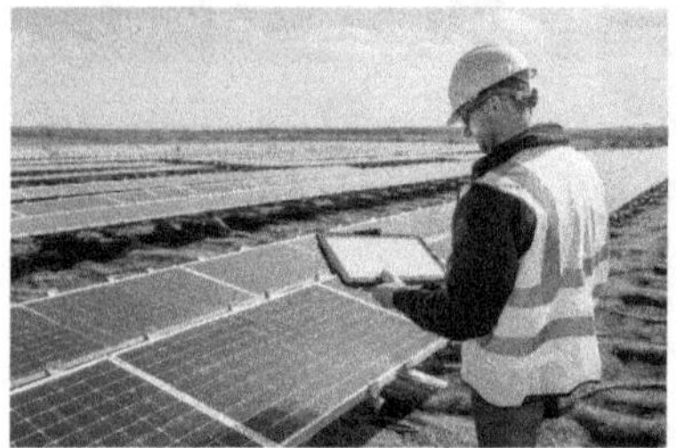

Your Location And Industries In Your Area

Let's face it, the going rate for drone services in Los Angeles is going to be much different than the exact same services in Detroit. Know your market and competition and don't overprice (or underprice) yourself. Give your client options with tiered packages that offer different sets of deliverables. If you target an industry that has little activity in your specific area, chances are that industry may already be saturated with drone service providers. That means not only will the stiff competition make it difficult to land jobs, but it will also make the price per job lower. Make sure there's room in your chosen area, or find something that differentiates you from the competition so you get the call.

Keeping these factors in mind when setting up your drone business will help you target the businesses and industries that are most likely to result in higher return on investment for your specific skills, equipment, and area of operations. Evaluating demand in your region, understanding current market trends, and keeping up with evolving regulations will also help you stay competitive as the industry grows.

As you gain experience, you might find areas that pay better and yield longer-term clients. Remember that how you present yourself, price your services, and communicate value can be just as important as your flying ability. How you approach these is what we'll cover next.

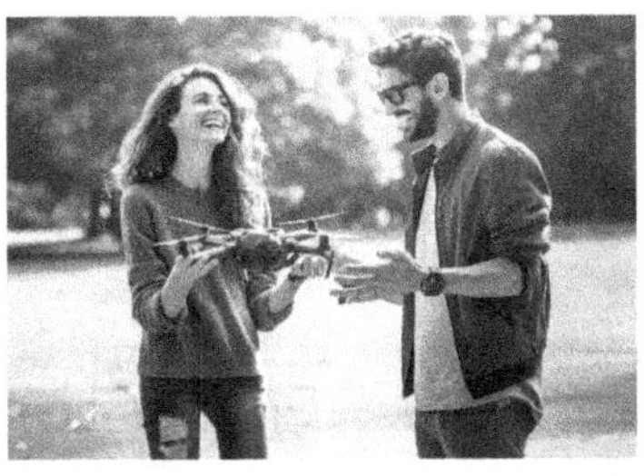

Chapter 4:
Startup Costs

"Flying might not be all plain sailing, but the fun of it is worth the price."

-Amelia Earhart

Starting any kind of business takes money, and running a drone service is no exception. Once you sit down and add up everything you'll need, from the drone itself to accessories, software, and insurance, you may realize the startup costs are higher than you first expected. The good news is that with smart planning, most of these expenses are manageable and can be scaled as you grow. The types of clients and industries you plan to serve will shape what you actually spend, but let's take a look at some of the most common costs you'll likely face when getting started.

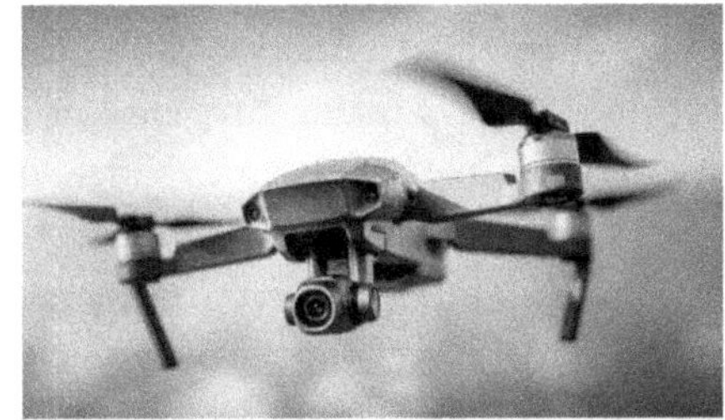

The Drone
$700-$20,000
or more

The single most important piece of equipment for your business will be your drone. And while the specific aircraft you need will depend on your target industries and goals, you should always plan with an eye on the future. Find a drone that will suit both your immediate needs and your near-future expansion plans as well. This is especially important in the U.S. where foreign-made drones and drone parts that are not on the NDAA list are now being treated as "national security risks". This effectively freezes introduction of new foreign-manufactured drone models and many foreign-made critical parts. It **does not** ban existing models authorized before December 22, 2025. In the UK, you'll now need to take a new "Flyer ID Test". You can find out about that here: https://www.caa.co.uk/drones/getting-started-with-drones-and-model-aircraft/prepare-for-the-flyer-id-theory-test/.

Buy What Makes Business Sense

When choosing a drone, don't get caught up in chasing the newest or flashiest technology. Many affordable models today can capture impressive images and video that would have cost many times more just a few years ago, and they may fit your business needs perfectly. Before spending large amounts on drones, batteries, screens, chargers, and accessories, take time to define your goals. Think about what kind of work you plan to do and how long you expect to use that specific drone. For example, a lower-cost drone may be great for real estate photos or basic roof inspections, but it likely won't have the advanced sensors and adaptability needed for high-end aerial cinematography. Matching your equipment to your intended market will save you money and help you grow at a sustainable pace.

Buying Used

Buying a used drone can be a smart way to save money—as long as you're careful. Just like with cars, many pilots upgrade to the newest model as soon as it's released, which means you can often find reliable older models at reduced prices. This can be an excellent option if you're just starting out or need a dependable backup drone. Always make sure you know exactly what you're getting. Stick with trusted sellers like B&H Photo Video, Adorama, or the manufacturer's own refurbished store, which often offers factory-tested drones at a discount. Confirm that the package includes key accessories such as batteries, chargers, and AC cords, and that the model meets your needs and current regulations. If buying from an individual, insist on testing the drone and reviewing its flight logs to make sure it hasn't been in a crash or suffered damage.

An Example

When it comes to residential real estate, a drone that costs $700 could be fine. But for Aerial Cinematography, there is a minimum standard expected, and the client's project will normally dictate the specifications of the drones you fly. In this case, your aircraft has to be flexible when it comes to cameras, lenses, formats, and color space as well as its ability to hold up in different production scenarios.

With ultra-high-end productions and for maximum shot flexibility, you might need a dual-operator configuration where a pilot flies the drone and a separate person operates the camera. In this case, your costs are increased exponentially because of the added crew and equipment costs. The drone itself can be upwards of $15,000-$20,000 or more, plus the need for a separate camera operator, a third crew member for tech & gear, and a possible fourth to act as Visual Observer. The ramp-up to competency for this class of drone is significant. Your logged time in this configuration should be high enough to where you feel just as comfortable as if you were flying alone on a single operator rig.

The bottom line is when it comes to what to buy and why, make sure you know your client-and don't make the mistake of chasing work with bigger and more expensive drones. Have a regular customer base to support it and a solid business and marketing plan in place. In most cases, the client will need a specific deliverable (not a specific drone). It's your job to figure out which tools can get that in the best way possible.

Minimum Drone Specifications

No matter where you choose to focus, your drone should have these minimum specifications:

-**Camera that captures 4K video (3840 x 2160) and 20mp still photos;**
-**Raw (DNG) Photo record capability;**
-**3-Axis Gimbal (pitch/roll/yaw);**
-**3-way obstacle avoidance (suggested);**
-**Ability to mount filters in front of the lens;**
-**A manually-adjustable shutter and frame rate (optional, but strongly suggested).**

To narrow your drone choices a bit, consider an online search using "Best Drones for _______" (fill in the blank with industry or year). The key takeaway is to buy the most drone that you can afford at the time-don't skimp. This is your most valuable tool and the key to making money in this industry. Do your research, determine your goals and figure out your target focus. This will take you a long way finding the drone that's right for you.

Before you head out on your first job, remember that buying a drone is just the starting point. There's quite a bit more you'll need to ensure your operations go smoothly and safely. Things like batteries, chargers, storage cases, and extra propellers can make a big difference in how often you can fly. And don't forget about essentials like memory cards for recording, landing pads, and maintenance tools. You'll also need to think about software for planning flights, processing your imagery, and even managing your clients and projects. All of these tools work together with your drone, turning a flying camera into a reliable business tool. Let's take a closer look at the other equipment and software you should consider as you get your new drone business off the ground.

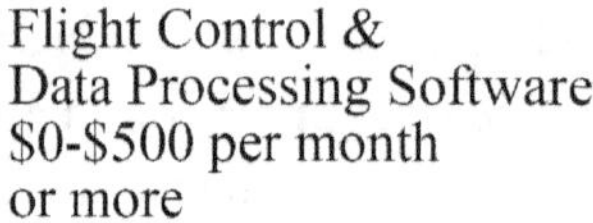

Flight Control &
Data Processing Software
$0-$500 per month
or more

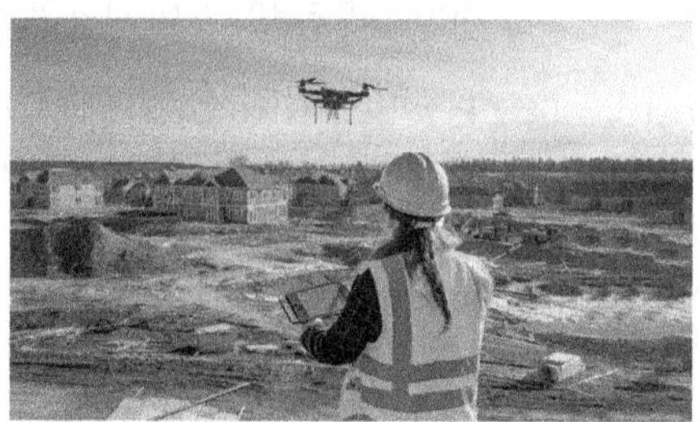

If you're flying construction sites, inspecting cell towers or wind turbines, or analyzing turf or crops, you're going to need one software to automate the flight and a second software to process it. In many cases, the data capture software is free; the processing is what's costly. Choosing the right software depends on several factors, including your project goals, level of technical experience, budget, and the types of files you need to output.

Prices range from free to hundreds of dollars a month. The paid solutions can be subscription-based or one-time purchases. Some are designed for specific industries such as agriculture, construction, or surveying, while others cover a wide variety of applications.

For construction sites, cell towers and wind turbines, you're normally automating the capture of still images that will eventually be stitched into your "Orthomosaic" map or 3D model. You can think of the "Ortho" as something that resembles a Google Map, but that has much higher resolution and is much more current (the images are processed into the ortho immediately after flying and uploading). For turf or crop analysis, the flight automation is normally the same, but the camera used to capture the images and the resulting analysis done by the software can be quite different and rather expensive. In addition, for topographic maps or if your client requires globally-accurate deliverables, you'll have to use ground control points or drones that correct positioning information in real time. I'll discuss these features and differences later when we talk about specific industries.

Data capture software companies include DJI Terra, Drone Deploy, Pix4D, Maps Made Easy, SkyCatch, UgCS, and others. Many have a trial plan that lets you try the processing software before committing.

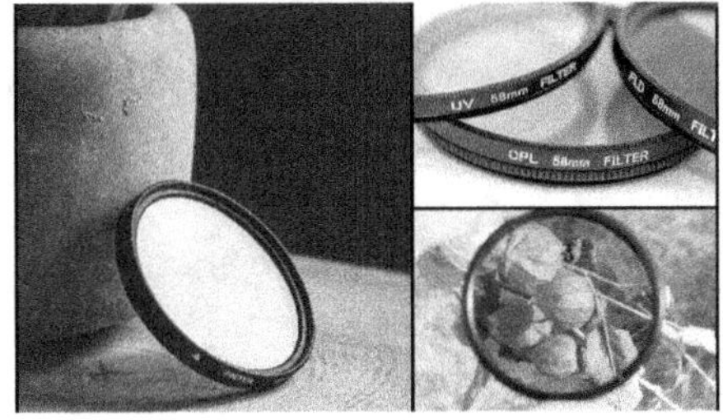

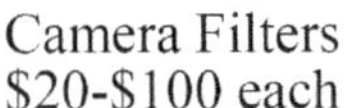
Camera Filters
$20-$100 each

Even many of the most basic drones allow you to install a filter in front of the lens. Filters change how much light reaches the sensor and can also affect the quality or look of your photos and videos. The most common types are Neutral Density (ND) filters, which reduce the amount of light so you can avoid overexposed shots; polarizers, which help cut through glare and reflections; and colored filters for creative effects. Some filters even combine features, like ND/polarizer hybrids.

When choosing filters, look for high-quality glass with lightweight frames. This keeps your footage sharp and won't interfere with your drone's gimbal. While these features might make the filter a bit pricier, it's usually worth it for the improvement in image quality and smooth gimbal movement.

Besides helping you get better-looking shots, filters let you control your shutter speed and work with the right frame rate for smooth video. Later in the book, we'll dive deeper into how to use filters for the best drone photos and videos.

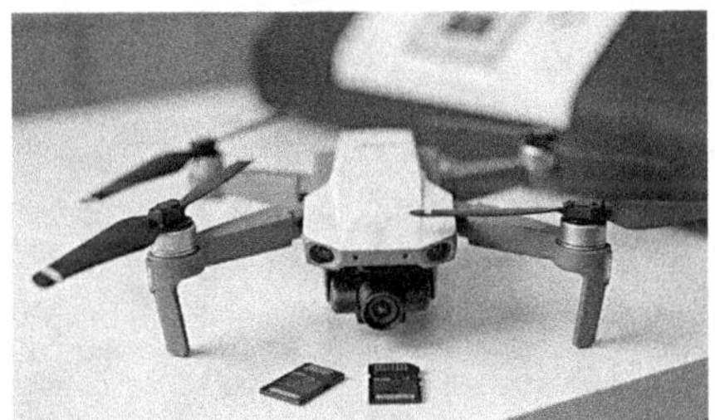
Recording Media
$12-$1,000.00

The higher your video resolution and frame rate—for example, filming in 4K at 60 frames per second—the more storage space you'll need to capture all your footage. It's important to check if your drone allows you to record to a removable memory card, like a microSD, instead of relying only on the drone's internal memory. Using removable cards means you can quickly swap in fresh storage and keep flying without interruption. If your drone records only to its internal drive, you could run out of space in the middle of a flight session and have to land just to transfer files before you can continue. This not only interrupts your workflow but could also lead to missed shots, especially when working under time or weather constraints. Bringing along several high-capacity, high-speed memory cards ensures you'll always have enough space for all your footage and prevents unnecessary stops during your mission. Always check that your memory cards are compatible with your drone's camera, and invest in reliable brands to avoid data corruption or loss.

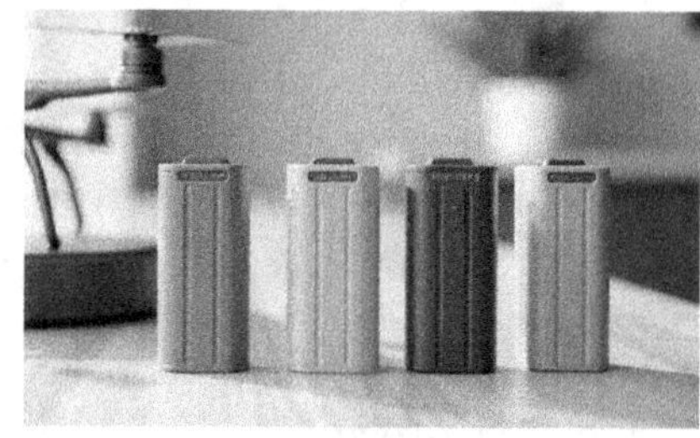

Extra Batteries
$55-$800

Battery technology has come a long way since I started flying when a typical flight would last 12-15 minutes. Now, flights of 30-45 minutes are commonplace. Buy enough to cover the work you'll be doing. If you fly a lot of full-day missions, make sure to have a sufficient battery count or a pre-planned charging routine to keep you going. Buy and use only those made or authorized by the manufacturer. Any short-term savings with off-brands could jeopardize your mission and cost you a drone in the long run.

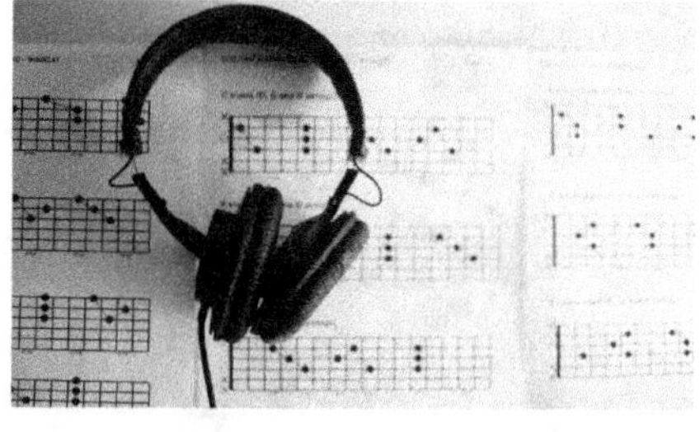

Music Licensing
$0-$20 per month
or more

If you're editing videos, you're going to need a good music library to pull from. A *very important* thing to remember is that "Royalty free" does not mean no cost to use, nor does it mean that the music is copyright free. "Royalty free" means you have the right to use copyrighted music without having to pay a separate fee each time you use it. There *are* some sites, however, such as Pixabay's music site where authors have given up their rights to the music and made it part of the public domain. This music is *totally* free. You cannot resell the music and there are certain restrictions on how you can use it, but for the most part it's a tremendous resource. Keep in mind that although there is no fee, you are still required to "license" the music and are subject to any stipulations of that license. A good rule of thumb is to read the licensing requirements for any site before downloading and using their music cuts.

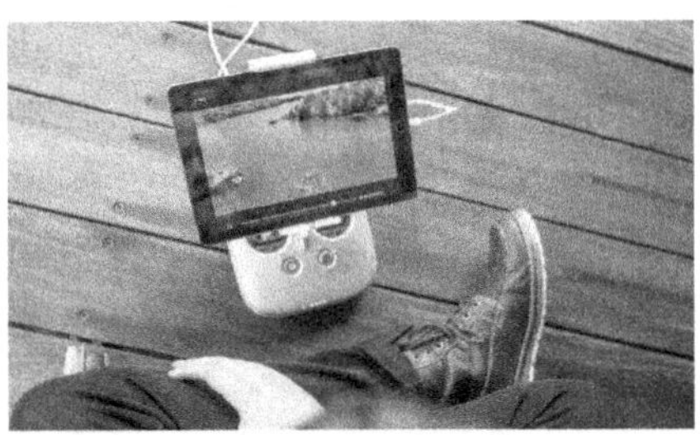

Screens & Monitors
$300-$1200 Each
Plus Extra Batteries

Some drone controllers come with built-in screens, but for those that don't, you have plenty of options. There's always your phone in a pinch, but it's small, unprofessional and not always suited for the job. For DJI drones, I use the 7.85" Crystal Sky, a high-resolution monitor that is also extra bright so you can see your shots in direct sunlight. Another popular choice is the iPad Mini, but it's difficult to see on bright days and tends to overheat and shutdown when it's hot. And don't forget a second, separate client monitor so your customer isn't constantly looking over your shoulder at the shot.

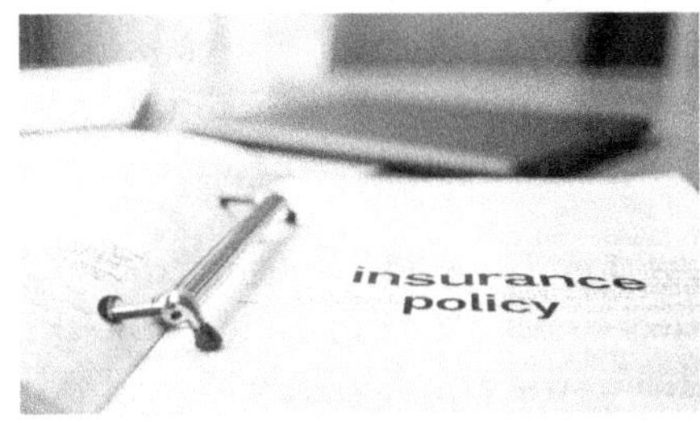

Insurance
$750-$2,000

You might be tempted to fly without insurance, but doing so can put you *and your client* on the hook for any damage caused by your drone during a mission. Skipping it could be a recipe for financial disaster in the long run. A $1 Million (US) drone insurance policy (sometimes called "Aviation Liability") is pretty standard, but some industries and jobs require a higher amount (especially construction). Drone liability covers the damage your drone does to buildings, objects and things on the ground-not the drone itself. If you want to insure your drone, that's usually called "Hull" insurance and pays to replace the drone when accidents or incidents happen. Depending on the drone, you may want to get a replacement policy from the manufacturer when you buy the drone, which is usually less expensive.

You should also consider business liability, worker's comp and an umbrella policy, especially if you're a sole proprietor. Business liability protects your business and actions of your employees or freelancers working for you. Worker's compensation protects not only your employees, but can also include freelancers and others you hire. For instance, when we fly in highly-restricted airspace, we are required to hire police escorts and their departments require us to cover them with Worker's Comp insurance. In the EU drone insurance is mandatory for drones over 25kg.

Editing Software
$0-$20 per month

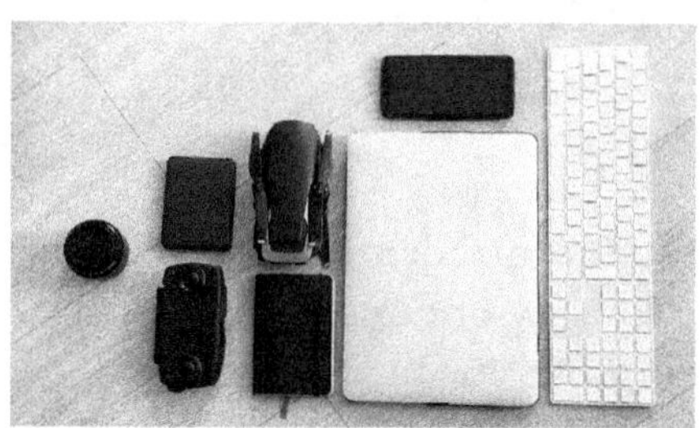

Many clients will request an edited video as part of your project deliverables, so it's a good idea to plan for this from the beginning. Editing could be as simple as creating a "progress" video, where you arrange photos and clips with background music, or as complex as putting together a polished production with graphics, narration, and custom soundtracks. At the very least, you should learn how to combine your shots into an overview video that tells a clear story. This single skill can make you much more appealing to potential clients and allows you to charge higher rates.

If you're not interested in learning the ins and outs of professional video editing, don't feel pressured to make it a central part of your services. Just remember, some clients will expect more advanced videos, so in those cases, partner up with a trusted editor who can handle complicated projects for you at agreed-upon prices.

For your own basic editing, you can start with free software like iMovie (great for simple edits), CapCut, or LightCut, which is designed for drone footage and offers one-tap editing features. Advanced free tools such as DaVinci Resolve give you more power for color grading and effects, while paid programs like Adobe Premiere Pro, Final Cut Pro, and Wondershare Filmora offer even more options for experienced editors.

No matter which program you choose, the key is to pick something you find intuitive and scalable as your business grows. Learning basic video editing not only expands what you can offer clients, it also makes your work stand out in a crowded field, helping your drone business thrive.

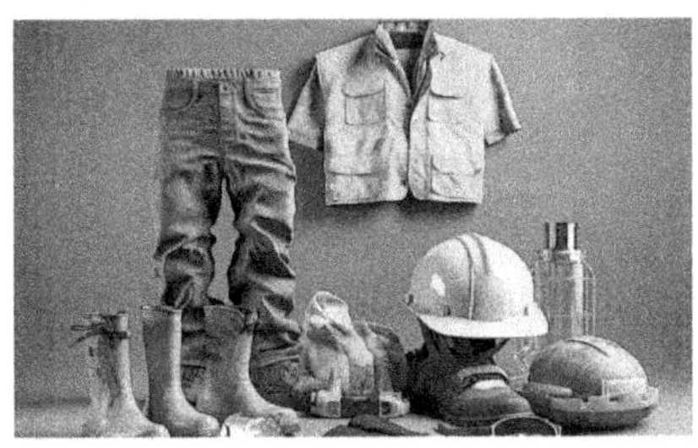

Specialized Gear
$150-$300 or More

If you're planning to fly drones at construction sites, safety gear is essential. Many jobs will require you to wear steel-toed or composite-toed boots, a hardhat, and a high-visibility vest. These items must meet specific safety standards set by the industry, so always check what's expected for your site.

Beyond these, you should also consider safety glasses to protect your eyes from debris, and protective gloves. Ear protection is smart if you'll be working around loud machinery. Weather-appropriate clothing, such as waterproof jackets and sun protection, can also be a big help for long days in exposed environments.

Other useful equipment includes a rugged carrying case for your drone and a reliable means of team communication like two-way radios or headsets. Staying organized and prepared not only keeps you safe but also helps you meet client expectations and keeps the project on schedule.

Freelance Pilots
$40-$75 per hour

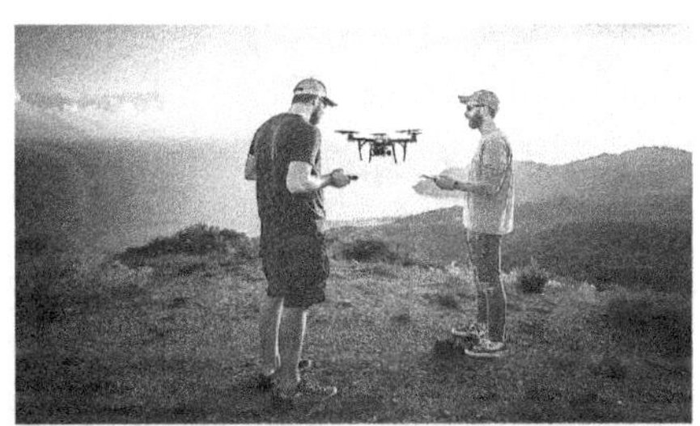

As your drone business grows, you'll almost certainly run into situations where you're double-booked or can't be at every job. That's when it helps to have a network of pilots that you trust. Make a habit of connecting with other drone ops that you meet at jobs, training events, or industry meetups; these relationships can evolve into valuable partnerships for sharing work and referrals.

When you have a schedule conflict, you've got a couple of ways to handle the overflow: you can refer your client directly to another pilot (and possibly earn a referral fee), or you can subcontract the pilot yourself and have them bill you for their work. Either way, the arrangement should be fair and clearly defined, so both parties benefit and know what's expected.

Set clear terms in writing for every collaboration. Be sure to cover payment, deliverables, responsibilities, standards, and confidentiality. These agreements protect everyone involved. Only refer or hire pilots whose professionalism matches your own; your reputation and your clients' satisfaction are on the line if someone drops the ball. And always make sure each pilot you work with has proper certification and insurance coverage to avoid any legal issues.

Strong pilot partnerships mean you have support when work piles up, and your colleagues will call you when they need backup, too. By building a trustworthy crew, you'll be setting yourself up for long-term success.

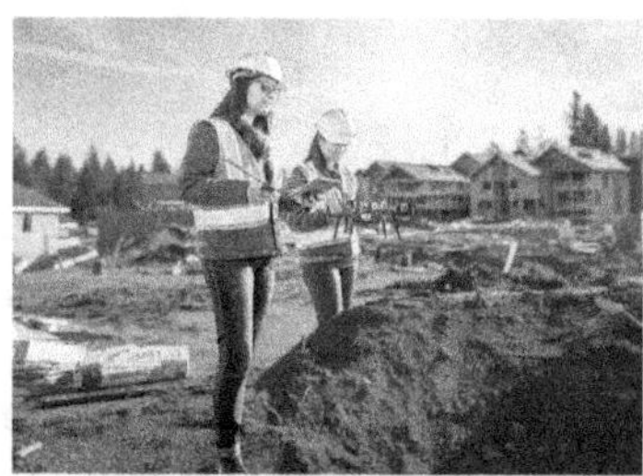

Freelance
Visual Observers
$20-$30 per hour

Even if you usually fly solo, there will be times when you need an extra set of eyes for safety, compliance, or added confidence. Sometimes, having a Visual Observer, or VO, isn't just a good idea—it's required by law, especially if you're flying beyond your immediate line of sight, using FPV goggles, or operating in complex or busy areas.

Don't wait until the last minute to find someone. Build a list of reliable VOs ahead of time—people you trust to help with critical safety tasks and clear communication. Up-and-coming drone pilots, even if they don't have a Part 107 license yet, often make great VOs because they're familiar with what to watch for and how to describe it. Friends and family can fill in occasionally, but make sure they understand what's expected: a VO must keep the drone in their line of sight, constantly scan for hazards, and *clearly* relay any potential risks to you, the pilot.

Have a quick briefing session before each mission so your VO knows exactly what you expect, how you want to communicate, and what to do if something unexpected happens. Make sure everyone knows the mission area, radio protocols (if used), and specific flight hazards. Don't forget that VOs can also help after the flight, noting any unusual conditions or problems that might affect your gear or future operations. Prepare well in advance, train your observers, and keep the lines of communication open.

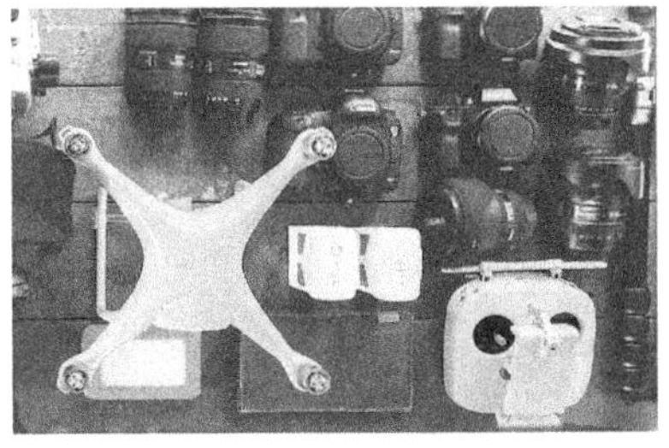

Miscellaneous
Equipment & Tools
$5-$600 or More

Accessories are necessities. Get a good case; preferably one with wheels. Make sure it holds all your batteries and screens and most of your main accessories. Splurge for water-tight. While you probably won't be flying in the rain, you might be wheeling it through mud and it's easier to clean if it's water tight.

Next, you'll need to recharge in the field. An inverter works in a pinch, but you're limited by the proximity of your vehicle and the wattage of your accessory plug. Even though your inverter may be rated at 500 watts, you can't run more wattage through it than your car accessory plug can handle-usually 110. A much better option is a portable generator such as the EcoFlow. It's like a big recharge-able battery with AC outlets and USB ports. It recharges itself with a conventional outlet, through your accessory port in the car or even with an optional solar panel.

Don't forget tools. Keep a small tool kit in your bag that includes everything from usb cables, super glue and gaffer's tape, to screwdrivers, batteries and lens cleaner. And I never leave home without a can of compressed air. It comes in handy for blowing debris off the lens or even for blowing cool air through your drone's cooling ports on a hot day.

Keep in mind, this is your business—every expense is yours to manage. There's no company supply closet to raid or office manager tracking what you use. You're responsible for keeping your equipment in working order, buying spare parts ahead of time, and making sure you have what you need to get the job done. It's easy to get tempted by every new gadget, but you don't have to buy the latest tech just because it's on the market. Focus on what truly supports your current work. You call the shots and cover the bills, but you also get to enjoy the freedom and rewards that come with being your own boss.

With careful planning and smart choices, you'll discover that the effort is worth-while; and the opportunities can be just as exciting as you imagined.

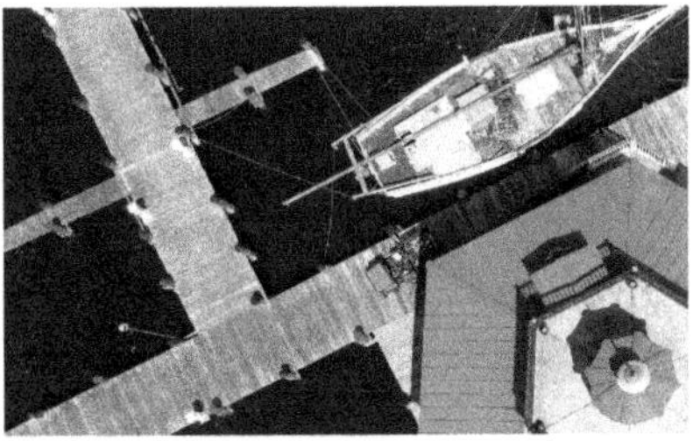

Chapter 5:
Still Photography

"Great photography is about depth of feeling,
not depth of field."

-Peter Adams

Drone cameras, sensors and lenses have advanced to the point where taking aerial still photos is no big chore. Fly the drone to the spot, take the picture and move on to the next task. With inexpensive drones taking 20 and 40 MP images, anyone can be an aerial photographer, right? I'll leave that for the pundits to debate. I maintain that, as with other endeavors involving some degree of creativity, the drone is simply a tool. In the right hands, it can seemingly do magic. But, to become that aerial magician, you've got to be familiar with some basics.

What You Need To Know

One of the most critical elements of aerial photography is *exposure* which is all about managing the amount of light in a photo so details are clear and colors look natural. Our eyes can distinguish more details in the shadows and highlights of a scene than a camera can record. In photography, this difference between the darkest recorded detail and the brightest is called "exposure latitude" or simply, "latitude". The greater the latitude, the greater the opportunity for capturing more of what our eyes see when we take the photo.

Exposure is influenced by three main elements known as the "exposure triangle": shutter speed, aperture, and ISO. **<u>Shutter speed</u>** controls how long the camera's sensor is exposed to light when you take a photo. The faster the shutter speed, the less light getting in. The shutter is the part of the aperture that opens and closes to let light in to the sensor. **<u>The aperture</u>** is the "opening" that controls how much light reaches the sensor during an exposure. A larger aperture has a lower "f-stop" number and lets in more light. A smaller aperture has a higher "f-stop" number and allows less light to reach the sensor. **<u>ISO</u> is** the camera sensor's sensitivity to light. You can increase exposure by lowering your shutter speed, opening your aperture or increasing your ISO. Each of these have their benefits and drawbacks.

The lower the shutter speed, the greater your chance of getting a blurry image due to subject or drone movement. Faster shutter speeds freeze motion; slower ones can introduce blur. You can use this to emphasize the motion of your subject. This can also be a desirable effect when you want to blur one portion of the image and not another. For instance, flowing water in a landscape or passing traffic in a street scene.

Aperture changes can affect your "**depth of field**" (the part of your image that is in focus at any one time). A larger aperture (smaller f-stop) can give you a shallow depth of field with only a small part of the scene in focus. A smaller aperture (larger f-stop) increases depth of field rendering more of the overall scene in focus. The "focal length" of your lens (how wide or telephoto it is) can also affect depth of field. Most consumer and lower-end professional drones have fixed focal length lenses that are very wide, so the aperture's affect on depth of field and focus is usually minimal in these cases.

A higher ISO lets you shoot in darker conditions but can reduce image quality because it isn't actually seeing more light, but rather amplifying the light signals that it detects—along with any noise that's also there.

Tools for Measuring Exposure

Your eyes aren't always a good way for judging exposure in a scene. Many drone monitors optimize the scene for viewing, and don't necessarily show how it's being recorded. That's why you should take advantage of the tools that come with your drone's camera to accurately measure the scene exposure.

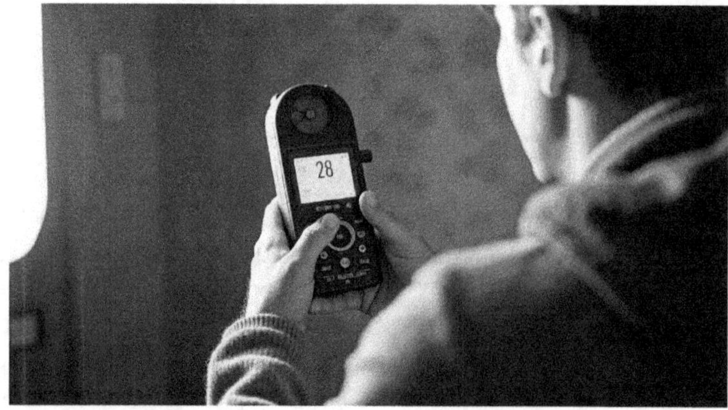

We don't have the luxury of lighting our scenes

"Zebras" are diagonal black and white stripes appearing over areas of the image that are close to overexposure or blown highlights. They only show up on your screen-not in the actual recorded image.

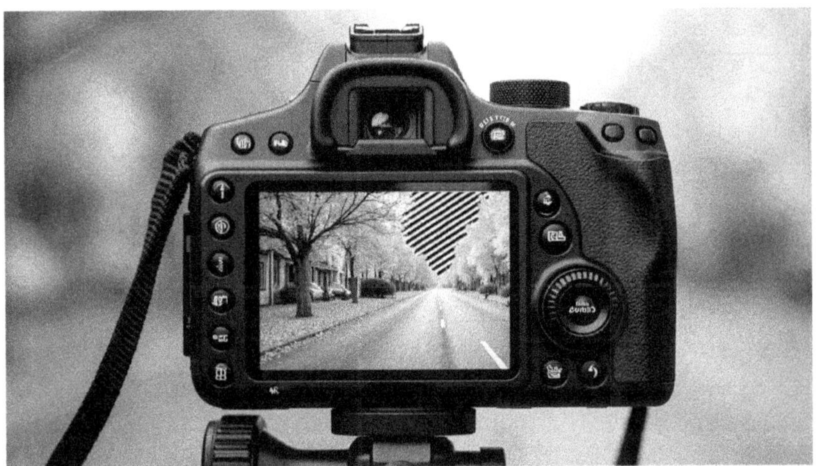

Zebras show areas in danger of overexposure

The zebra pattern indicates areas where the brightness exceeds a set threshold, often between 75% and 100% brightness, signaling that those areas might lose detail if the exposure isn't adjusted. Zebras may be adjustable or fixed, depending on the manufacturer. Know your zebra settings and use them regularly.

A **Histogram** is a graph that shows the distribution of brightness levels in a scene, ranging from dark shadows on the left to bright highlights on the right. It helps you see if the image exposure is balanced—with most tones spread evenly—or if parts are too dark or too bright, which means details may be lost. In drone photography, histograms are especially useful because lighting conditions can change quickly due to altitude, weather, and reflective surfaces like water or rooftops.

Using zebras and the histogram during drone flights lets you be aware of what you're capturing, but sometimes you might have an extremely high contrast scene where the difference between the shadows and the highlights is too great for your camera's sensor to capture. In that case, you run the risk of under- or over-exposing your subject. Once that happens, there's not a whole lot you can do to make the image look good. Artificial Intelligence ("AI") might work, but the preferred solution is to shoot your stills in a "RAW" format. Most drones list this option as "DNG", although you may see "ARW" or "NEF" for SONY or Nikon cameras.

RAW files are larger than traditional JPEGs and preserve a wide dynamic range and color detail, giving you much more flexibility to adjust exposure, white balance, shadows, and highlights during post-processing without losing quality. RAW is like a digital negative, ideal if you want to carefully edit and enhance your photos later.

JPEG files are compressed and processed in-camera, producing smaller files that are ready to use immediately with some loss of detail and dynamic range. JPEGs are faster to transfer and easier for quick sharing or printing but offer less freedom to fix an image after capture because much of the image data is discarded. If I have a quick turnaround without time to process, I'll use my drone's "bracketing" feature and then use AI to combine the best-exposed parts of each shot into one composite photo. "Bracketing" is when you take multiple shots of the same scene using different exposures. In this case, the drone does it automatically and fast enough so that the three different exposures are essentially the same shot. To combine them, I normally use "Luminar NEO" and it works like a charm.

Other Considerations

White Balance and Color. White balance is a camera setting that adjusts the colors in a photo to make white objects appear truly white, regardless of the lighting conditions. It compensates for the color temperature of the light source—whether warm like sunlight or cool like shade—to ensure that colors are rendered naturally and accurately.

For drone pilots, white balance is important because lighting conditions can vary widely depending on time of day, weather, altitude, and reflective surfaces such as water, snow, or buildings. Proper white balance ensures that aerial photos record true colors. Incorrect white balance can cause unwanted color tints (e.g., too blue or too orange), reducing the image quality and making post-processing more difficult.

While many drone cameras have white balance presets (for instance "sun", "shade", "night", etc), I find it better to use the automatic setting. You should be cautious when shooting at times such as sunrise and sunset where you want the vibrant colors of that time of day. Your auto setting may try and make it look like a mid-day scene. Shooting RAW will alleviate this problem.

Using Filters. A rule of thumb I have is to always have a filter on your lens. This keeps dirt and dust off the lens and protects it from damage. Never wipe the surface of your lens with anything. If necessary, use compressed air to blow any contaminates off the surface. Most drones ship with a clear filter attached to the main camera. Keep it there. Many times this is an **Ultraviolet or "UV"** filter that blocks unwanted UV light that is more of a nuisance to film cameras than digital.

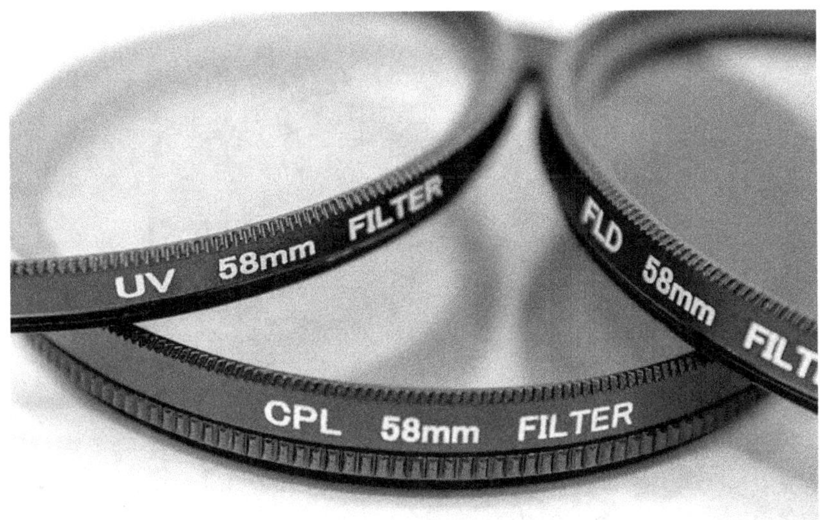

Filters also protect your lens from dirt and damage

Neutral Density or "ND" filters reduce the amount of light entering the camera lens without affecting color. This is especially helpful on a bright summer day or with snow scenes. They are essential when shooting video which we'll cover in the next chapter.

Polarizer filters ("PL" or "CPL") reduce reflections and glare and enhance color saturation and contrast of a scene. They also help clouds and blue skies stand out. They are sometimes combined with ND filters and indicated by "NDPL". Regular polarizing filters can interfere with digital camera sensors and focus, so make sure to use the ones marked "CPL" for "Circular" polarizer. Circular polarizers are designed to work smoothly with today's digital cameras.

Some polarizing filters have to be rotated to get the best angle for photos. Spin the filter while watching the image on your screen until the desired amount of polarization is dialed in.

Basic Post-Production Tips

To get the most out of your images, you might have to process them after capturing. Little things like cropping to improve composition, adjusting exposure, correcting colors and white balance for natural tones, and sharpening can make a big difference and add value for your client. But to do that, you'll need software.

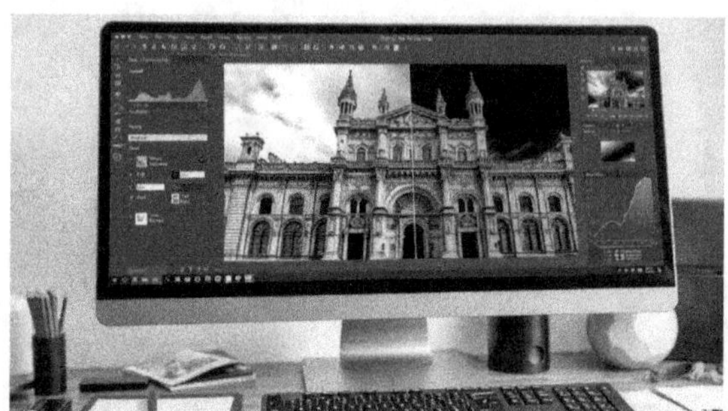

Familiarize yourself with photo editing software

There are lots of beginner-friendly options, both free and paid. Adobe **Lightroom and Photoshop** are popular paid choices with lots of tools for color correction, exposure adjustment, and organizing photos. If you're familiar with Adobe products, you'll be at home with the interface and AI options. For free software, try **GIMP** for easy adjustments, and **Darktable** as an alternative focused on RAW image processing similar to Lightroom.

For AI-powered standouts, **Aftershoot** is a good choice for culling and batch editing that learns your style to speed up sorting and color adjustments. Adobe Lightroom has a AI-assisted tools, and **Luminar Neo** has simple AI-driven features like portrait touch-ups and sky replacements that are quick and easy with great results. **Topaz Photo AI** specializes in fixing noise, sharpening, and recovering details with minimal manual input, which can be helpful for rescuing images taken in challenging lighting situations. Many of these also have free trials or different levels of pricing.

In the next chapter, we'll go further as we look at the basics of shooting video and how to get the best moving images from your drone.

(Note: The author receives NO compensation for mentioning any of the products in this book).

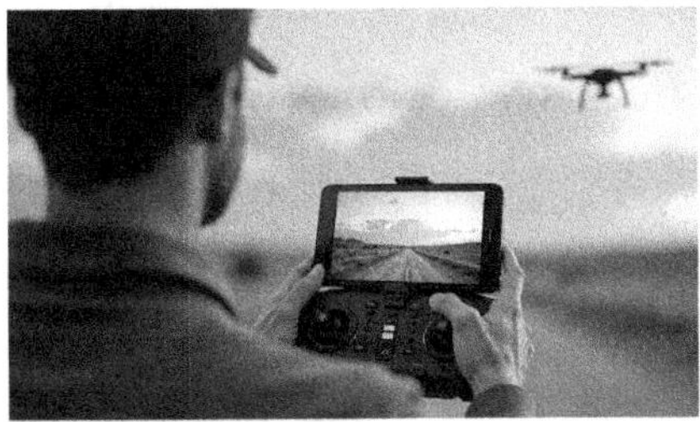

Chapter 6:
Video Basics

S hooting drone video can be fun and lucrative, but there are a few things you should keep in mind in order to be successful shooting video with your drone. Everything we've learned in the previous chapter about still photography still applies, but now we have the added complexity of having to pilot the drone while capturing moving shots. (Note: this chapter assumes your drone has a single operator; the pilot also runs the camera.)

Most importantly, remember that you are flying a sophisticated piece of aerial equipment. Safe and responsible flight should always be your top priority to protect people, property, and your investment. Be aware of and follow all laws and regulations for the airspace you're operating in, and never fly recklessly. Of course, this applies to whether you're shooting stills or video, but with video, you'll tend to be more distracted while trying to fly the aircraft, watch for obstacles, and successfully get the shot all at the same time. Now, let's talk about aerial video.

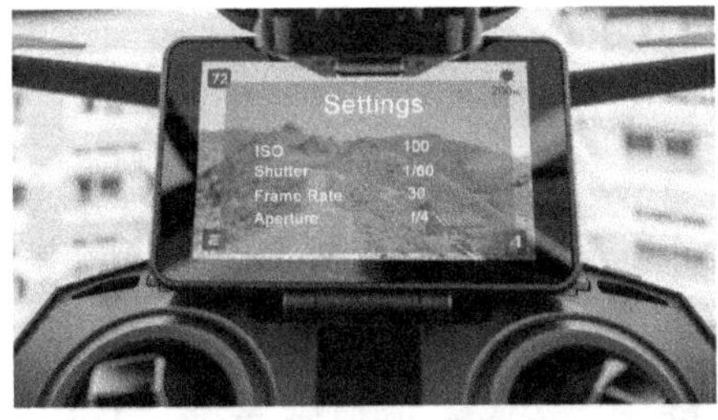

The Technical Stuff

When it comes to shooting video with drones, many of the techniques and settings we learned in the previous chapter for photography still apply, although some take on new importance for moving images. There are also key, video-specific elements you'll need to focus on to capture professional-looking footage. For instance, the lowly filter. Many beginning drone pilots don't realize this relatively inexpensive piece of equipment is essential to recording quality video images. Yes, they can change the quality of light to make clouds pop out and reflections disappear (as a polarizer does, for instance). But, more importantly, filters also allow you to align your frame rate and shutter speed to avoid "jittery" video (one large role for the ND filter).

Frame Rate, Shutter Speed and "Persistence of Vision"

Persistence of vision is where the human eye retains an image for a brief moment even after the actual image is gone. This is what makes a rapid sequence of still images appear as smooth, continuous motion to our brain. In video and film, it is responsible for allowing a series of still frames to blend together, creating the illusion of fluid movement rather than flickering images. This is how video & motion pictures work: each frame lingers on the retina just long enough to connect with the next one, so our perception fills in the gaps and sees ongoing motion. Without it we would see individual, disjointed frames instead of one moving picture.

What This Means to You

To create smooth, natural-looking motion, you have to set the shutter speed to roughly twice the frame rate. This means if you're shooting 30 frames per second (fps), you need to set your shutter speed to 1/60th of a second. When synced properly, the slight motion blur captured in each frame matches how our eyes expect to see movement, smoothing the transitions from frame to frame and enhancing the illusion of continuous motion. If you don't sync, your video will be either somewhat muddy (too slow) or jittery and choppy (too fast).

Color Space, Codecs and Resolution

Many beginning photographers (and new drone pilots) confuse color space, codecs and resolution. Here's what you should remember.

Color Space defines the range and relationship of colors that can be represented in an image or video. It determines how colors are captured, encoded, and displayed, making sure it's across all devices. The most well-known is "Rec.709".

A Codec is a method or algorithm used to encode, decode, and compress video. It affects file size, quality, and compatibility. Examples include H.264, ProRes, and HEVC.

Resolution is the number of pixels in each frame of video or in an image, typically expressed as width × height (e.g., 1920×1080-HD or 3840×2160-4K). Resolution determines the detail and clarity of the image but not how color or compression is handled.

Logarithmic

As we discussed in the previous chapter, with still images, you'll probably be increasing your recorded exposure range (dynamic range) by shooting in a RAW mode (usually designated by "DNG" on drones). In video, however, and with drone cameras in particular, you'll most likely increase your exposure latitude by capturing video in Logarithmic or "Log" mode. Log is normally designated under "color space" and can be D-Log (DJI), S-Log (Sony) or any other variation depending on the manufacturer of the camera you have. Log is not technically a "color space", but rather a profile used to record video with extended dynamic range. It captures a flat, desaturated image that preserves highlight and shadow detail, which can be color graded later to achieve the look you want or need. While it's definitely a valuable resource, it requires you to have a thorough knowledge of post production to be useful. It cannot be used right out of the camera without first applying some sort of color grading.

Plan Your Shots

When capturing video, keep in mind that you're not just taking one picture, you're taking 30 pictures *every seconds* (for 30 fps). Your shot is constantly moving and changing, and to have it be useful, you've got to know where you're starting, where you're stopping, and how you're going to get there. Every shot should have a goal and a plan to get to that goal.

For instance, if you want to capture a truck dumping a load of dirt on a construction site, think about what you want and need to see then think about how you can best capture that.

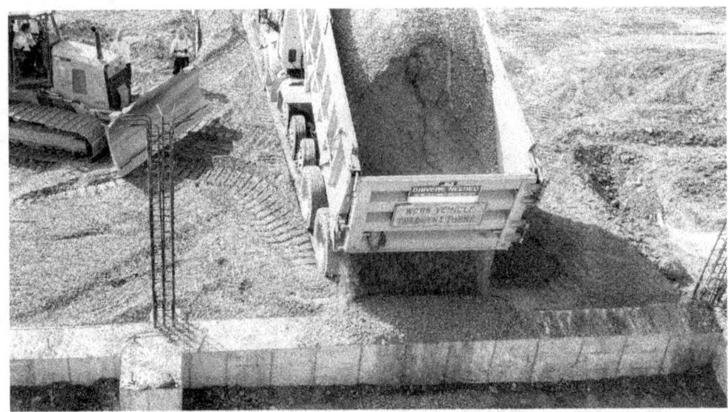

Plan your shots

Does the shot start with the drone following the truck and continue through the dump? Does the truck enter frame and then the drone moves with it? Does the truck exit the frame at the end of the shot or does the drone push in to the dirt pile? Does the drone start wide and fly into the truck already dumping its load? Does the drone fly lower ("Ped Down") as it moves closer to the dirt pile? How does the shot end? A script or Director may dictate many of these decisions, but as the pilot, you are responsible for executing the shot and providing complete sequences, not just random shots.

General Tips

Pay Attention to Light. With drones, we don't normally have the luxury of lighting our subjects, so we have to depend on natural light. Try and avoid shooting in the middle of the day. Midday sun is harsh and flat. Morning and evening light is soft and pleasing with a desirable angle. Side light helps to model your subject with shadowing.

Roll Early and Keep Recording. When capturing a shot, don't start your move right after you've pressed record. Hold a couple of seconds before you start your move and keep recording a few seconds after the shot ends. Your editor will thank you later. Once you start a shot, commit to following it through. You may want to try a second take, but stopping in the middle of a shot because you see something else more interesting will result in two shots you can't use. Finish what's in front of you and then move on.

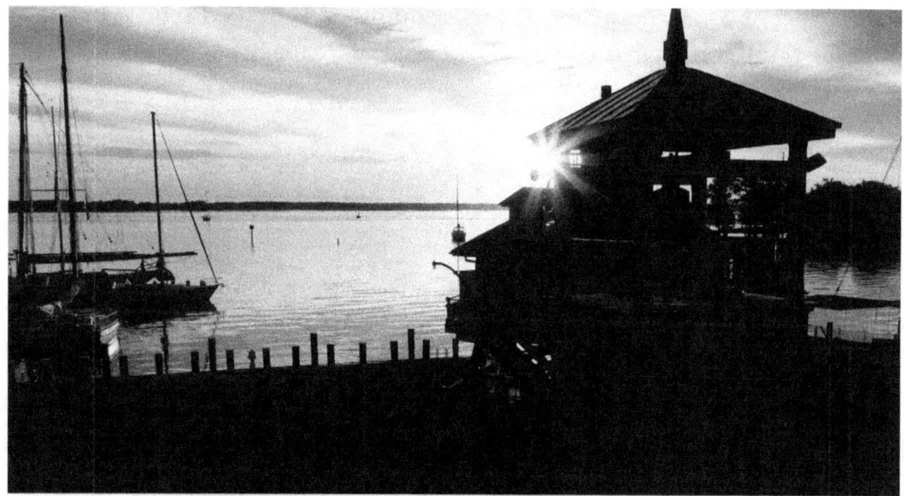

Side reveals work well with sunrise and sunset shots

Foreground movement is dynamic. When framing video shots, *get close to things.* Foreground objects close to the drone add a dynamic element to your shots and make them interesting. Wide shots from high above are good for establishing and have their place, but you won't go wrong if you think *foreground*. This is especially true when filming **sunrise & sunset shots.** I like to set my exposure so that the sun is exposed properly, which puts any foreground subjects in silhouette—and I like to have foreground movement. Try starting with a foreground object blocking the sun and then move off of the object to reveal the sun.

This makes for a dramatic and striking shot (known as a "side reveal"). This also works in the daylight. Just make sure your lens and filters are clean because any little speck will be very noticeable and probably show up in your image.

See examples of these shots on my website: www.MikeSobola.com/resources.

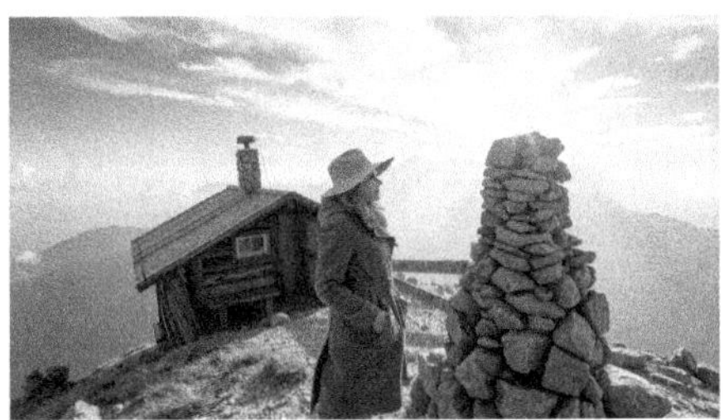

If you're shooting very large objects, try and include something in the frame for scale; a vehicle or person, for instance. Otherwise, your subject can end up looking like a scale model rather than the impressive landscape or piece of architecture that it really is.

Opposing Movement. Opposing movement in video is a creative technique where the camera or drone moves in one direction while the subject or foreground elements move in the opposite direction. For instance, the drone rises from low to high as the camera tilts down. Another example is the "parallax" shot: while the drone moves sideways in one direction, the camera pans or yaws in the opposite direction. This results in the foreground and background layers moving differently, adding visual depth and interest.

Opposing movement creates a more dynamic, layered look in your shots. It draws the viewer's eye through the frame, making them more polished and engaging. You can also use it to focus attention on a subject, or to provide a smooth reveal of a landscape or object. It takes some practice to learn to "see" and fly it, but once you master it, you'll see the difference it adds to your finished video product and the options it opens up in the editing room. We'll discuss that more in-depth in the next chapter.

Here are some other useful moves you should know:

- Hover: Keeping the drone in one position for an extended amount of time. Great for graphic treatments such as credit rolls.

- Orbit/Arc: Revolving around the subject while keeping it in the center of the frame. A partial orbit would be an "Arc".

- Ped up (Ascend) or Down (Descend): Flying up or down while keeping the subject in the middle of the frame.

- Ped Up with Reveal: Starting out with one subject in frame and flying up (ped up) to reveal another subject behind the first.

- Fly in or "Push": Moving the drone towards the subject.

- Fly out or "Pull": Backing the drone away from the subject.

- Slide: Flying the drone left or right without moving the camera.

- God's Eye/God's Eye Reveal: Looking straight down at the subject. For reveal, ook straight down with the subject out of frame. Fly left, right, away or towards the pilot to bring the subject into frame.

- Ground Reveal: Camera starts looking at ground or water and tilts up to reveal subject. Very dynamic when drone is moving forward toward subject

- Combo Reveal: Drone pushes in and flys down while raising the gimbal/camera until the subject breaks the horizon line, attracting your attention to it. This is a complex "three finger" maneuver that takes practice but is very effective.

- Pull Reveal: Drone pulls back to reveal more elements to the scene.

For video examples, go to my website at www.MikeSobola.com/resources.

Once you get comfortable with the individual moves, try and combine shots to make your videos even more dynamic. Experiment and practice-you'll find your favorites!

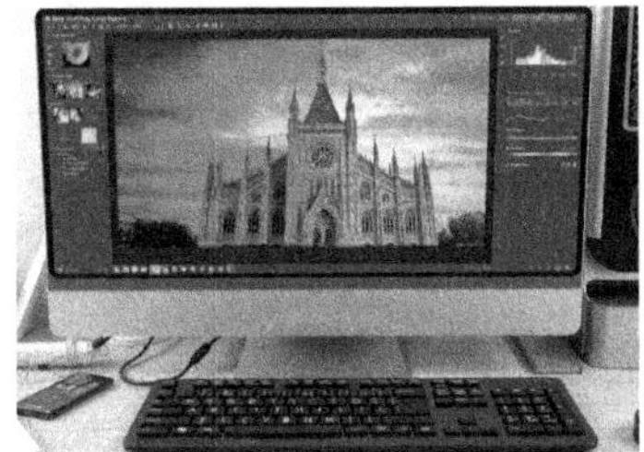

Video editing is an essential skill for drone pilots, because at some point, you'll have a client who wants you to edit their video. And rather than lose them as a customer, you'll want to know how to give them what they want. Offering your services as an editor is an "upsell" that can increase your profit margin quickly.

Becoming proficient quickly is a matter of finding software that's right for you and your projects. If you're cutting construction progress videos set to music, for instance, you won't need as many bells and whistles as if you're putting together a promotional reel for a new restaurant. And your learning curve for the former will be a lot smaller than the latter. While "how to edit" is beyond the scope of this book, we do have a few tips to help you incorporate editing into your workflow and make any editing you perform be quicker and easier.

Choose the Right Editing Software. Find a software that works for you. You'll want one that's intuitive and easy to learn and has some sort of support mechanism such as video tutorials and an online community. Some free options include DaVinci Resolve, Shotcut, HitFilm Express, Movavi, and even iMovie. Paid software includes popular brands like Adobe Premiere Pro, AVID, Canva, CyberLink PowerDirector, Final Cut Pro and Wondershare Filmora. Take the time to learn the basics such as proper importing, cutting, adding transitions, using music & sound effects and exporting the final piece.

Be Organized. Capture the footage in a logical way so that it makes editing the clips easier later on. When I'm shooting construction progress for a client, for instance, I start at one point and work my way around the building in a logical manner. A regular routine helps ensure that I don't miss anything. Once I get back to edit, I'm familiar with where the shots are based on when they were shot. Sometimes, I rename the clips and put them in an order that makes sense to me and the project. SomeThen I archive the project so that it's easy to find in case the client wants changes down the road.

Structure the Story. Every piece is a story, whether you know it or not, It needs a logical beginning, middle and end. For a building, we may start at the front, make our way over the roof to the back and end up showing a wide shot of the air handlers in the back. Find the logical "story" in your piece and work your way from the beginning to the end in a way that makes sense.

Don't ignore pacing and rhythm. Editing has a lot in common with music, especially when it comes to pacing and rhythm. Your piece shouldn't be one long, loud video that you slap a piece of music on at the end and call it a day. Let shots establish and play out, but don't let them linger.

Choose Music Wisely. Music should be selected and laid down first if possible. That way, you can let the rhythm help edit your piece. cut to the beat or "feel" the natural cut points where your shots want to start and end. And don't just pick one track and lay it down the entire length of the piece. Sometimes this will work, but for the most part, music should enhance the flow of the piece. It should function to introduce new "thoughts", accentuate important points (in the visual or the narration) and punctuate and "button up" section ends. This is even true if you have no narration. Remember-every piece tells a story in some way or another. Use your music to help tell that story.

Find a Good Music Library. And with music, you really do get what you pay for. For me, I prefer the stock site "StoryBlocks" (www.storyblocks.com) which also offers music clips. Another popular one is "Pixabay" (www.pixabay.com/music). As I mentioned in a previous chapter, **"royalty free" does not mean no cost to use, nor does it mean that the music is copyright free.** "Royalty free" means you have the right to use copyrighted music without having to pay a separate fee each time you use it. (On Pixabay's music site authors have given up their rights to the music and made it part of the public domain. This music *is totally free*.) A good rule of thumb is to read the licensing requirements for any site before downloading and using their music.

Natural Sound is Your Friend. "NATs", as it is commonly known, is not usually captured by a drone, but your piece will be greatly enhanced by adding it. If you have it, use it. That shot of the guy with a jackhammer is crying out for noise. Put it in and make the viewer happy. Most music libraries have a sound effects section that you can search. Don't overdo it, but when the piece screams for some extra "noise", be sure to add it.

Keeping these basic editing tips in mind will help you elevate your pieces quickly without a tremendous learning curve or ramp up.

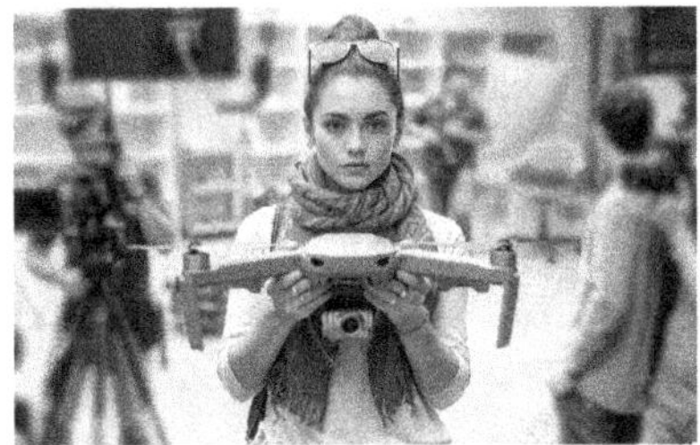

You can't get work without experience; you can't get experience without work. And while you do need to know the basics of flying and have some time under your belt before you can expect to get work, this catch-22 that we all run into actually has a way out.

Aggregators

Take a look at what I call "aggregators" to get practical training flying in real situations. "Aggregators" are companies that sign up drone pilots across the country and around the world then advertise a large presence. For some aggregators, it works this way: They get a request for a drone pilot and if it's in your area, you get an alert and can accept if you're fast enough (it's usually not exclusive). For other companies, the client needing drone images posts their job details with location and price. You can accept the rate or counter-bid with your own rate. Either way, the aggregator is doing the marketing and advertising for you. You just need to sign up and complete your profile on the sites. The upside is that it's easy. The downside is it doesn't usually pay that much. Some of the better-known outfits include: Drone Hive, Droners.io, and ZeitView. There's a more comprehensive list in the "resources" chapter at the end of this book. While you won't as much as if you got the job yourself, you'll gain confidence and get paid while you learn.

Watch and Learn

Another way to gain experience is to work as a Visual Observer, or "V-O" with an established pilot. At Mid-Atlantic Drones, we're always looking for good VOs and any of the freelance pilots we hire have come from the ranks of those who've previously served as VOs for us. You'll be able to learn from someone with more experience by working closely with them. It's the perfect way to establish a working relationship and demonstrate your dependability to someone who may have work to throw your way in the future. The pilot you VO with may have a higher price point threshold for taking jobs than you do, which means you can make it clear to them that you'd gladly accept any missions that they might otherwise turn down. Just make sure you send a thank you or, better yet, a finder's fee to them for referring you. Think of it as a sales commission on work that you wouldn't have gotten if they hadn't sent it your way.

Study Your Own Work and Others'

When you're not in the field, take the time to study the work of other pilots. Find a couple of good ones whose work you admire and watch their online videos. See the types of shots they get and pay attention to how they edit their videos. Notice what they include and what they *don't* in their pieces. Take note of how the shots start and end and how fast the drone is flying. Then add any new shots and moves to your list of things to master. Look at your own work with a critical eye and work on problem areas. Better yet, have others critique your shots and give you an honest and specific assessment. The only way you can get better is to work on the things that you need to improve.

Find a Cause

Many new pilots find that volunteering their services for a cause can be rewarding not only for the experience, but also for the value you bring to the organization. Make your time and equipment available for search & rescue operations, low-budget independent film work and "spec" ventures (where a sale is not guaranteed and you get paid when the project sells). My daughter works with animals so I regularly get calls to help search for a lost dog or cat, and I often worked on interesting independent films when my schedule allows. These projects allow me to stay connected to the production world, keep my flying skills sharp and to "give back" to my community.

Consult

Further down the road when you've got some experience under your belt, become a "go-to" speaker for drone and airspace information by volunteering for industry panels, speaking engagements, and consultations with volunteer and student organizations. Let news organizations know that you're available to speak when drones are in the news. The exposure and the people you meet often lead to paying work down the road, plus you're building community connections and earning lots of good will.

Practice Maneuvers and Online Learning

Early in your career, you'll be doing lots of flying for no other reason than to practice-and that's normal. Make a regular schedule of it, just as if you had a paying gig. Find a few flying spots in uncontrolled airspace that have different features (hills, lines, trees, water) and use those to work on your flying skills. (See links to specific practice maneuvers at the end of this book.)

When the weather's too bad to fly, pull out your laptop and look to the internet where your online learning options are almost limitless. You can sign up FREE for LinkedIn Learning courses (previously Lynda.com) through your local library and take advantage of photography, videography and drone courses there. You'll need a library card from your local library, the library's LinkedIn Learning library code, and your specific PIN number linked to your card that you get from your library. Then do an online search for "LinkedIn Learning for library" to get to the login page. Enter your info and, Bang! You're in. Specific details can be found on the "Make Use Of" website at:

https://www.makeuseof.com/tag/lynda-com-free-library.

Of course, searching the internet for "drone online learning" will pull up hundreds of YouTube videos and training programs; pick one that works for you.

Nothing Beats Experience

Remember-the best training is experience. You're going to make mistakes. When you do, just make sure you learn something from them. Early in my career, I was flying in the mountains of Nevada where the winds up high can be treacherous. Flying out, I neglected to notice that the winds were behind me, which gave me a stiff headwind on the way back. Eventually the drone self-landed in the desert (unreachable) among the cacti and rattlesnakes. It's still there. Now, I'm keenly aware of winds and weather. If I'm flying in windy conditions, I keep an eye on my power and set my battery alarm higher so I have enough juice for a safe return home. Plus, I'll always try and plan so my final leg home has a tailwind whenever possible. A tough lesson learned.

Getting over the catch-22 of work and experience isn't easy, but you can do it with a little creative thinking and a lot of hard work.

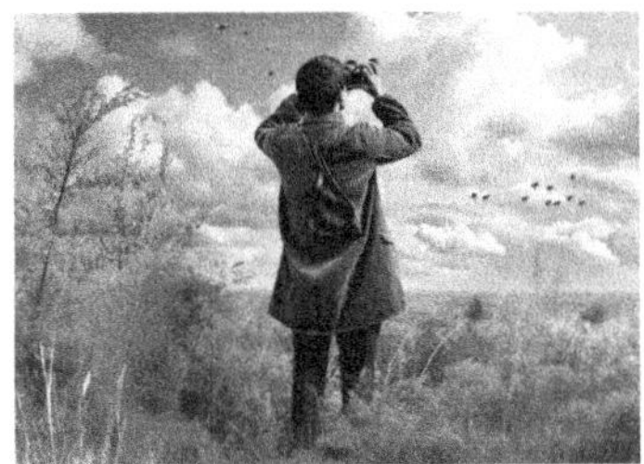

Chapter 9:
Finding Clients

There's an old saying that goes, "Build a better mousetrap and the world will beat a path to your door". Not quite true, I'm afraid. If you build a better mousetrap (or drone business), nobody's going to be knocking on that door of yours unless they know you're there and they trust you to do the job. You build that trust and knowledge through marketing.

Marketing vs. Selling

Marketing is not the same as selling. Marketing sets the stage for selling by creating awareness and generating leads and includes promoting your service or brand to your target audience. For your marketing to be effective, you have to understand your customers' needs and wants, create strategies to reach a potential customers, and build awareness and interest in your services. Marketing usually happens before any selling begins. Key elements of marketing include Market Research, Product Development, Branding, and Public Relations. Let's take a brief look at each of those.

Market research is gathering information about customers, competitors, and market trends to identify target audiences and market opportunities. How? Read industry trade media and learn what's new. Follow your potential customers to find out what they post. Review competitors' web sites and social media posts. In the same way you find out about your customers through their socials, you can also figure out where your competition thinks it's important to be by watching them online, too.

Product Development grows out of market research to create and refine your drone services so they align with customer needs and desires. To do this effectively, you must first know who your target customer is. It goes hand in hand with Branding.

Branding is probably the most difficult element here. It's what makes you different. To be successful, you've got to come up with a unique identity and image for your product or company to differentiate it from your competitors. Ask yourself what sets you apart from everyone else. That's your brand identity.

And let's not forget about **Public Relations**. This is managing your brand's reputation and public perception through media relations, community engagement, and other communication efforts. Earlier, I mentioned gaining experience by volunteering as a speaker or working with community organizations. This builds good PR through community engagement and word-of-mouth and you'll be doing some good for the world.

Niche Down

So, how do you find your specific focus—your "brand"? There's a saying that goes, "Jack of all trades, master of none". Nowhere is this truer than when you're flying drones for a living. With experience and flight time, you can certainly grow to cover a wider range of areas and industries that you service, but, when starting out, it's important to focus your energies on smaller market segments. This allows you to become good in a few areas as opposed to mediocre in lots more. Maybe you've decided to target Aerial Cinematography as your focus. That's great, but you've only just begun to focus. As with other target industries, Aerial Cinematography is too broad a category to target effectively on its own. All top-line categories (such as Construction, Real Estate, Agriculture) can be further niched down into more-specific specialties.

How to Narrow Your Focus

As an Aerial Cinematographer, for instance, you could specialize in independent feature work, or corporate video productions, nature and outdoor video, or extreme sports. Start with something you know, that you are connected to, or that might be a natural extension of what you do now or of an expertise you possess. For instance, if your background is in construction, Construction Drone Imaging would be a perfect start for you. If you're an architectural photographer or videographer, Aerial Cinematography for commercial real estate would be a great extension of your business. Are you a volunteer firefighter, paramedic, or other first responder? You can probably see the value of aerial imaging for search & rescue or accident investigation. Weigh the pros and cons and come up with the right business model for you. Be clear on what you do, how you do it and why you're different from your competition. Then go out there and show 'em.

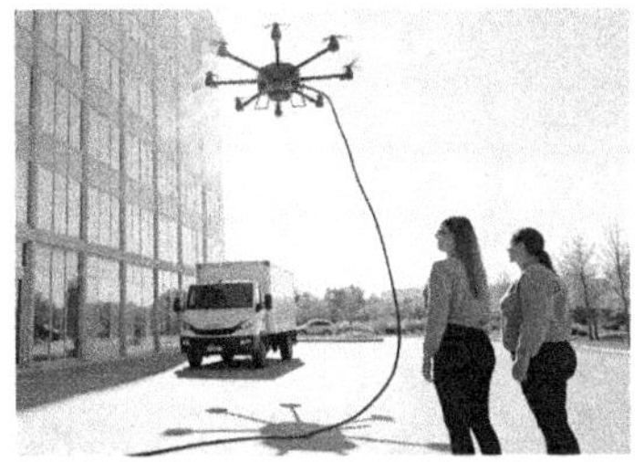

"The way to get started is to quit talking and begin doing."
-Walt Disney

While aerial photography and videography is what many new pilots dream of, the truth is, there are plenty of less-glamorous areas that need and want drones. Flying drones has developed into quite a robust service industry from aiding in construction and development, agriculture, real estate, inspection, disaster recovery and more. But, some say that the "revolution" in Artificial Intelligence is making drone pilots obsolete, especially with the onslaught self-flying drones that companies can operate with non-pilot teams. The good news is that, at least for the majority of operations in the US., you are still required to have a licensed drone pilot supervising missions. As a drone pilot, you can try and snag one of these supervisory pilot positions, or you can start thinking bigger.

Drone Automation

The real play is supplying and running the entire system that these companies want and need. Because, while the sales pitch by manufacturers and sales reps is all rosy, the truth is, you'll need special expertise to work with these "self-flying drones". Drone automation is standard standard fare in the construction and inspection industries, among others. But real value comes from automating your entire mission cycle: from flight planning and autonomous flight with data gathering, to data upload & analysis and report generation. With a "drone in a box", it's getting easier to do.

What You Need

If you're using the system, you'll need the drone, a base station and highly-specialized software. The base station, or "box", is the aircraft "hangar" acting as a charging station and launch/land platform. The mission software is the "brain" that manages the aircraft and its missions while also collecting and analyzing the drone's data for further use. It's the central hub where missions are programmed by an operator who might be managing multiple at the same time.

Specific Drone Systems

Here are some of the autonomous "drone in a box" systems available (in alphabetical order):

Autel Robotics: Offers the EVO Nest system with EVO Max series drones, with autonomous deployment, charging, and AI tracking with the "SkyCommand" Center.

DJI: "DJI Dock" is typically used for industrial inspections, security, and surveillance with automated launch, landing, and charging controlled by the DJI FlightHub.

DroneMatrix: A European manufacturer of drone-in-a-box systems designed for BVLOS missions with remote control rooms. Its Aerial Robotic Work System (ARWS) is the backend that programs and controls the drones and collects the data for analyzing.

Easy Aerial: Military-grade drone-in-a-box systems for defense, border control, and critical infrastructure with fully autonomous operation after deployment. NDAA Compliant and listed on the DIU's "Blue" list.

FlytBase: Offers a backend "orchestration" platform and tools to use with many of the drones mentioned above. It is hardware agnostic so you can tailor it to your needs or (as a service provider) configure it to work with your customers' current and compatible drone fleet where desired.

Percepto: Autonomous drone-in-a-box platforms for industrial inspections and remote site monitoring with AI-powered decision-making and minimal human involvement. Of all the players in this space, Percepto seems to be one of the best positioned due to its advanced AI-enabled data analytics.

Skydio: The Skydio Dock pairs with Skydio X10 drones, giving you full remote site monitoring and inspections without on-site pilots.

XRT Drone in a Box: Fast battery-swapping docks compatible with DJI Matrice 30/350 series and Autel EVO Max, featuring 5G connectivity and environmental monitoring.

How to Break In

According to Instagantt, a well-organized autonomous drone program can go from concept to operational status in about 6 to 18 months, depending on regulations and the technical expertise you have. Plus, it can be expensive and intimidating. As a drone pilot, your plan should include becoming a system designer that looks at a company's requirements and puts together a system best suited to their needs. The plan should address how many systems they will need, the necessary software (and license seats where applicable), a rollout strategy, and training for their staff. If they have no drone program, this could mean a total solution from one company (drones, box and flight software to program, control, monitor and collect the data). If the company is already using drones, look at pairing their drones with a compatible flight hub program. FlytBase is a great solution in this case due to its AI analytical capabilities in addition to the initial flight planning and execution phases.

More than likely, you'll be offering this as a service and provide your customer with a total plan based on their specific needs. Your price should include all equipment and your fees for getting it up and running and a transition period for handover to their staff. You'll also want to build in some sort of retainer option for when they want you to come in on an "as-needed" basis. Remember, once deployed, these "boxes" stay in the field for extended periods of time and are normally dedicated to a specific *area*.

New Opportunity Areas

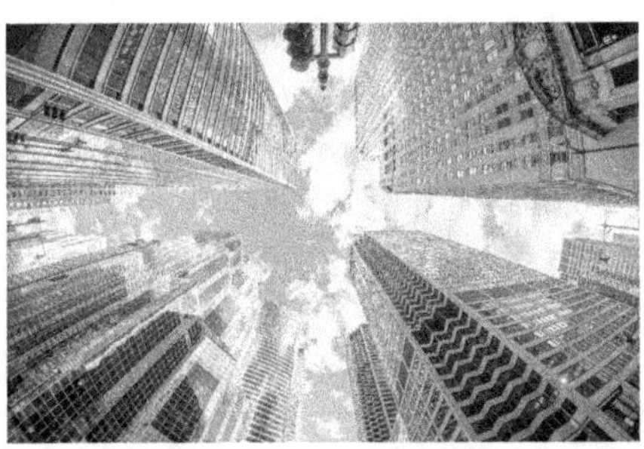

Window and Façade **Washing.** This area has been growing fast and furiously. Using special "cleaning drones" with water sprayers, hoses, pumps, and cleaning solutions, these drones clean high-rise buildings and windows without scaffolding or ropes and ladders. It's safer, cheaper and, should do the job in half the time.

Required Equipment

Expect high startup costs ranging from $25,000 to $80,000 just for equipment, depending on the drone numbers and size, payload capacity, and accessories. And that doesn't include any specialized training, accessories or extra insurance. You'll need a special spray drone, a ground-based water tank and booster pump system and cleaning solutions. You might also consider a drone with advanced navigation and obstacle-avoidance systems because you'll be flying close to buildings and obstacles. In addition, you'll need to haul all that extra gear around. That means larger trucks, trailers, and even employees (or freelancers) to do it right. Franchises are a great option here to help with business plans, marketing and suggested equipment.

Industry Trends and Future Outlook

Drone washing is a hot market that's buzzing with excitement. Everyone seems to be talking (or joking) about it. Funny chides aside, a committed entrepreneur can make some serious cash here with some forecasts predicting a surge to over $515 million by 2030. High-volume operations can gross up to $1m per year with a 30% profit margin (a $300,000.00 profit). Keep in mind, a high-volume business like this requires extra pilots, VOs, drones, and equipment plus schedulers and bookkeepers back at the home office. I would think a one or two-person operation can expect more along the lines of $150k-200k gross for a $45,000-$60,000 annual profit based on a 30% margin.

How to Break In

It's possible to get started with complete franchise programs that provide everything you need to get off the ground (pun intended). The franchise route usually offers a proven track record with training, marketing and equipment support, but requires a significant investment. The value of that investment can be a steady return and profits with a tested business model that they train you to run. Estimated startup costs vary greatly due to the different options available and requirements of each franchise deal.

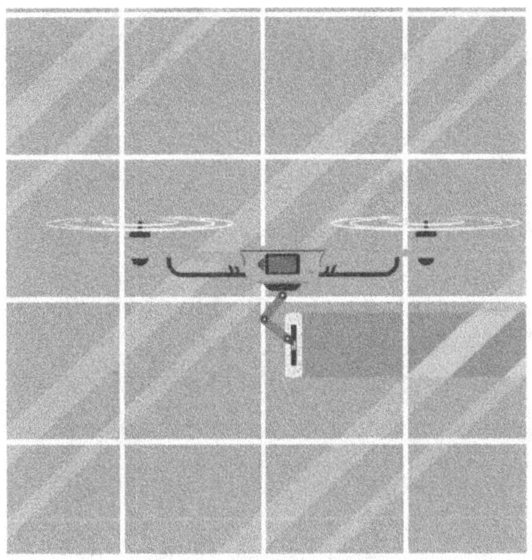

Cleaning Drone Franchises

Here are four companies offering franchises for drone washing. We have not vetted these companies and their inclusion here is not an endorsement of any kind. As with any business decision, perform your due diligence before investing any money with these or any other companies and make sure to comply with any franchise laws in your state or country.

Drone Wash. Describing themselves as "America's #1 Drone Cleaning Company", Drone Wash has a US-based franchise program for commercial drone cleaning, including window washing and exterior building cleaning. They've grown with the service, offering drone washing since 2021 (before it was cool). They can give you hands-on training, marketing support, and exclusive territory rights. See them here: https://www.trydronewash.com/franchise-benefits

WashDrones. Provides what looks like a complete turn-key franchise model focused on "cleaning at heights", especially for high-rise buildings and solar installations. Based in Australia, but franchising around the world. Their website: https://washdrones.com/franchise/

KTV Working Drone. This Norwegian company operates with drones they designed themselves that feature proprietary operating software specifically designed for washing, inspecting and coating (think spray painting). They have a very strong training and support system that screens potential franchisees to "boost their chances of success". If you go with them, you get access to their secret autonomous drone technology and the help to build your business locally. Find them here: https://ktvworkingdrone.com/franchise/

Drone Ops Cleaning Solutions. This Eastern US company advertises a couple of affordable options for potential franchisees. They have low initial down payments available structured so that part of the initial franchise fee comes out of your earnings until it is paid in full. They provide training, all equipment—including a trailer—and offer real time support six days a week. Get more details here: https://droneopscleaningsolutions.com/

Some typical costs associated with a drone cleaning business:

Equipment Item	Typical Cost (USD)	Notes
Specialized cleaning drone	$15,000–$45,000	Lucid Bots: $20,000–$40,000; Apellix: $40,000–$69,000; Aqualine: $15,000–$30,000;
Advanced spraying/cleaning payload	Often bundled or $5,000–$10,000 extra	Includes nozzles, pumps, and water delivery system
Backup batteries & charging system	$2,000–$5,000	Four batteries common for field longevity
Repair kit and parts	$500–$2,000	Usually included with high-end platforms; for quick field repairs
Ground-based water tank & pump	$2,000–$8,000	Required for deionized water and supply at high pressure
Cleaning solution and eco-safe chemicals	$500–$2,000 (stock)	Bulk initial purchase; ongoing cost
Controller (with live video)	$1,000–$2,500	Often comes with the drone, professional grade controller recommended
Navigation/sensor (LiDAR, radar, etc.) suite	$5,000–$10,000	Advanced models are bundled, crucial for obstacle avoidance
HD camera (for inspection/documentation)	$500–$1,500	May be built-in (4K cameras common)
Safety signage and ground barriers	$200–$1,000	Protects worksite and public
Licenses, permits, & insurance	$2,000–$5,000+ annually	Necessary for commercial flight and liability coverage

Energy Infrastructure Inspection

Many of us are used to Artificial Intelligence or "AI" programming our drones for more efficient flight paths, but did you know it can also turn our drones into self-learning machines and provide more efficient data analysis? This is especially true when it comes to energy infrastructure inspection. These inspections have traditionally been very time-consuming and dangerous—plus the assets have to be taken off line to be inspected. Now, we can use new drones equipped with special sensors like high-resolution cameras, thermal (infrared) imaging, LiDAR, multispectral sensors (for crops and fields), and ultrasonic wave generators for testing metal integrity. These inspections cover solar panels, wind turbine blades and towers, power lines, substations, energy tanks and more. They can find solar panel hot spots, wind turbine blade cracks, lightning protection faults, vegetation encroachment, structural defects, and gas leaks that might cause operational inefficiencies or safety risks.

What You Need

Solar panel inspections require thermal cameras and sensors to find malfunctioning areas or hot spots. Basic thermal jobs can use a drone with a cheaper "non-radiometric" sensor that shows temperature differences of roofs, walls and windows, for example. These types of inspections are common to determine where heat is escaping from buildings or windows and where roof leaks may be originating. You don't need any training to use these cameras, but you might want a basic knowledge of thermodynamics. Many thermal drone operators have a "Level 1" Thermal Certification that covers basic thermodynamics, thermal camera operation, and common applications like maintenance and condition monitoring. Level 1 operators know how to best capture thermal images and identify general problems, but don't normally interpret the data. In contrast, you'll need a *radiometric* thermal camera/sensor to determine precise temperatures. Radiometric thermal cameras measure and record absolute temperatures on a pixel level meaning they are perfect for any subject that needs precise readings of differential temps like solar panels.

If you decide to go the extra mile and provide *interpretation* of the data, you'll need specialized training or just let AI do the work for you. **Volateq Web App and MapperX** are two platforms that automatically find defects (hotspots, PID, disconnected strings, etc.) on thermal/RGB data.

For Wind turbine inspections you'll need a drone with a high-resolution camera and telephoto lenses. In some cases, clients might require LiDAR for in-depth blade and structure inspection and 3D modeling. Plus, you'll need the specialized flight software to go with it. Flight-controlling software includes DJI Flight Hub 2, Propeller Aero, Skydio 3D Scan, and Drone Deploy. Regardless of which drone you fly, you'll also have to upload your images to a "wind-specific" analytics platform like SkyVisor, Scopito, and Averroes AI.

Power line inspections combine many different sensor types (high-res optical, thermal, UV) to find faults, corrosion, and thermal hotspots. If you're flying around high-voltage lines, you'll want a drone that's shielded from electromagnetic interference (EMI) to prevent problems with communication, control, and recording software. More than likely, you'll also want a Beyond-Visual-Line-of-Sight ("BVLOS") waiver to fly long stretches of power lines over the course of your inspections.

Gas line inspections are very costly because of the highly-specialized sensors needed to detect leaks. These can be upwards of $100,000 each, not including the cost of the aircraft. Most gas line companies use their own internal employees and resources to inspect their lines.

Here's a comparison of common costs for drones and sensors:

Energy Sector	Drone Type / Features	Sensors Required	Estimated Drone Cost (USD)	Notes on Sensor Cost
Solar Panels	Multi-rotor drones, stable hover capability	Thermal / Infrared camera (e.g. Wiris Pro)	$5,000 - $25,000	Thermal sensor adds $5,000-$15,000
Wind Turbines	High-end drones with extended flight time	Visual + Thermal Infrared + LiDAR optional	$8,000 - $50,000	LiDAR sensors and thermal cameras increase cost significantly
Gas Lines	Long endurance fixed-wing or hybrid drones	Gas leak detectors, visual cameras	$15,000 - $40,000	Specialized sensors can add $50,000+ depending on technology
Power Lines	Multi-rotor drones shielded from Electromagnetic Interference (EMI)	High-res optical, Thermal, UV sensors	$15,000 - $40,000	Thermal and UV sensors typically add $5,000-$15,000.

Industry Trends and Future Outlook

Helicopter or manned aircraft inspections have been standard, but they're expensive and capture less detail than drones. Drones improve access, slash inspection times, and deliver better-quality data. In 2025, drone inspections were becoming standard practice, supported by automated flight planning and AI-powered defect detection. And regulations have been easing to allow previously forbidden ops such as BVLOS.

How to Break In

Solar. Your best approach is to target companies that own, manage, or maintain solar farms and residential or commercial solar panel installations. These companies include solar energy providers, renewable asset managers, solar installation firms, and facility management companies. As we mentioned earlier, you should consider specialized training or courses in solar drone inspection to increase credibility. This would include Level 1 Thermographer. Starting small with local solar businesses or residential installers and building a portfolio of detailed inspection reports can lead to contracts with larger energy companies or farm operators in the future. Offering convenience, safety, accuracy, and lower costs compared to manual inspections are the key selling points. Be ready with a plan and specific examples on how they can save time and money.

Wind Turbines. Here, drones are used for detailed rotor blade inspections, lightning protection checks, and tower assessments, replacing dangerous helicopter or rope access methods and cutting costs while increasing fault detection rates. to find business, you're going to have to do some cold calling. You can 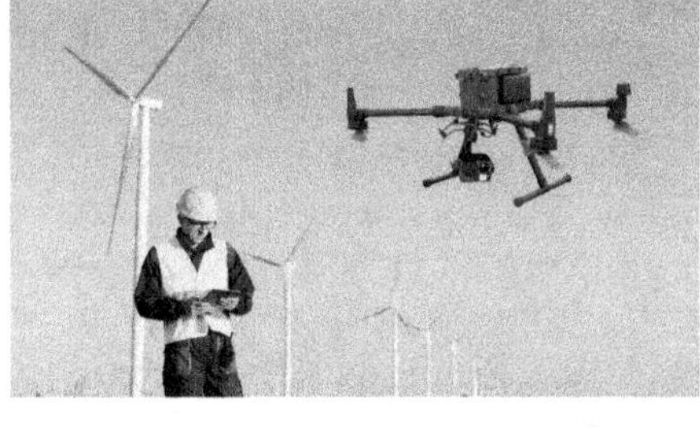 buy lists from https://renewables.digital (also lists solar contacts) to identify wind farm locations and then research the operators connected to those projects. Contact specialized maintenance contractors and service providers like Applus+ USA or ATS (Applied Technical Services), which offer wind turbine inspection services and potentially subcontract drone inspections. Go to windfair.us to find lists of business-related services and maintenance companies.

Power Lines. This is a tough area due to the specialized knowledge and equipment needed to do the work. If you've worked in this sector and know the technical side, you have a leg up. Otherwise, check with utility companies; some of them offer training for their specific operating procedures with drones around power lines including mock-up power stations and de-energized power lines for practice and training missions. Companies potentially needing this service include utility companies managing transmission and distribution power lines, energy providers and their subcontractors and other drone service companies that subcontract power line inspections.

Crop Spraying

If you know about farming, you're probably aware of "Precision Agriculture" and how it's really starting to take hold. It's been used the last few years for GPS-guided tractors and satellite-mapped crop dusting and seeding from traditional aircraft, but, according to a study in *Frontiers Plant Science*, drones make it cheaper, more precise, and complete the agricultural cycle that includes field analysis and planning, soil and crop health, and pest control. Drones can reduce waste and increase efficiency between two and five times over manned aircraft and ten times that for "on-the-ground" application.

For pure acres-per-hour, manned aircraft usually remain faster than spray or seeding drones on big, open fields, but drones can be more "efficient" in terms of chemical use, targeting, and usable work windows on smaller or irregular fields. For aerial seeding, planes and helicopters still win on raw coverage rate, while drones gain efficiency by reducing overlap, drift, and access constraints, especially on small blocks or sensitive areas.

Drones can break the barrier to entry wide open...Mostly. I say "mostly" because even with the proper equipment and knowledge, you'll still need special permits to use the chemicals. And that can be a real pain point for drone operators with no background in farming. If that's you, your best bet may be to partner with a farmer or specialist already in the field. Or structure your operations in teh beginning so that your client holds the permits and you do the calculations and fly the drones.

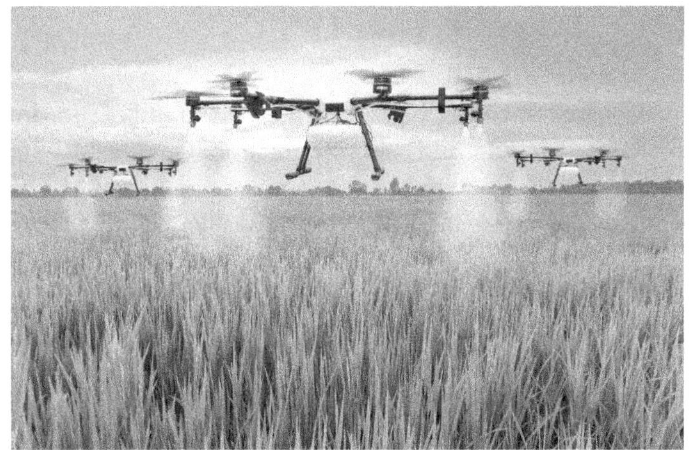

Crop spraying can be lucrative but requires special permits

Required Equipment, Software and Permits

To play in this space, you'll need spray drones with increased payload capacity fitted with special chemical delivery systems. These specialized drones are developed and manufactured specifically for this purpose. You'll also need mapping software to automate your flight and coordinate the spraying and flow rate with the fields. Some recognizable software companies include: DJI Agriculture and UgCS (for operational and spray planning) and DroneDeploy, Pix4Dfields, Agremo, and Sentera (for crop and field analysis). As you start to explore, you'll see that there's a bit of crossover in software between the crop health sector and mapping because of the common methods used to capture the data for both areas.

Industry Trends and Future Outlook

According to the American Farm Bureau Federation, the average U.S. farmer using drones can realize a return on investment of $12 USD per acre for corn and $2 to $3 per acre for soybeans and wheat. Labor shortages and a "sustainability movement" is helping drone operators get their foot in the door because of accuracy, precision and efficiency. Crop spray drone services have strong growth potential for you if you have the right tools and training, as more small and midsize farms open up to drone data and services.

Major Players

The leading software companies for drone crop analysis and ag spraying focus on advanced analytics, mapping, and spray automation. Commercial drone operators and farmers use these for crop health monitoring, mapping, "prescription" generation, and efficient spraying. Here are some leaders (in alphabetical order):

AgEagle. Drones and software for field imaging, spraying, and workflow management.

Agremo. AI-driven analytics focusing on plant counting, weed detection, stand counts, and pest identification with automated report generation—integrates with DJI drones.

DJI Agriculture. Operational software for planning, automating, and executing spray missions, compatible with the DJI Agras series drone.

DroneDeploy. A leading cloud-based platform for real-time field mapping and crop analysis.

Farmonaut. Software to pull together and analyze data gathered from satellite and other (drone) sources. Works with multispectral, thermal, and optical imagery in an "agri-platform".

FlyPix AI. Combines your images with AI analytics for advanced crop monitoring with precision.

Pix4Dfields. Field-ready mapping, instant prescription map creation, and advanced analytics, including weed and pest detection; supports most commercial drones.

Sentera. Real-time NDVI and advanced crop analytics directly integrated with both their own and third-party drones.

Trimble Ag. Drone management and data analysis, including integration of drone data for spraying, seeding, and crop assessment.

UgCS. Built for complex terrain and corridor mission planning (think pipelines and power lines). Supports both mapping and spraying with high-precision automation.

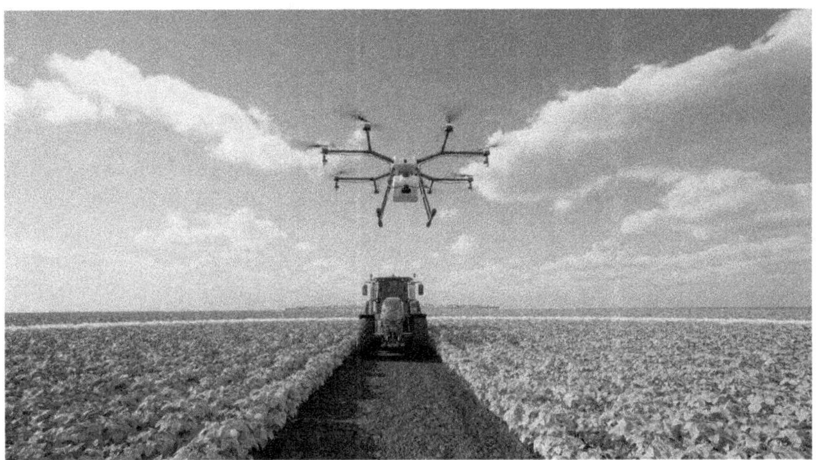

Spray drones increase efficiency on smaller farms vs traditional aircraft

How to Break In

Partner with someone who has an agriculture background who can help you navigate the farming side of the equation. If you plan on going it alone, you'll need to study up on crop analysis, field erosion, and soil health. You'll also have to know how to program your drone to fly a map and you'll need a crop spray license to buy and dispense any chemicals from your drone. Oh, and you'll need a couple of drones: one to fly and collect NDVI and RGB data on the field and crops and the other to do the spraying once you figure out what's wrong. For precision spraying, you'll also need separate software (such as "SmartFarm") to program the drone's flight path and the spray pattern for accurate chemical application. Choosing the right drone depends on farm size, terrain, payload needs, and local regulations. DJI and XAG lead in global adoption, while Hylio and Rotor cater to North American markets with local support and scalability. Be sure to consider payload, flight time, automation features, and compatibility with farm management platforms when selecting your equipment.

Spray Drone Manufacturers and Models

Turn the page for an alphabetical, non-comprehensive comparison of some leading spray drone manufacturers.

Manufacturer (Country)	Key Models	Spray / Payload Capacity	Primary Use Cases	Notable Features
ABZ Innovation (Europe)	ABZ L30	30 L spray tank	Medium to large European farms; operators needing EU compliance	Dual GPS, swappable tanks, designed around European regulatory and CE requirements
DJI (China)	Agras T40, T50	40 L spray tanks	Large farms needing high-capacity spraying	Dual atomized nozzles, advanced obstacle sensing, terrain-following, and integration with SmartFarm precision-ag platform
	Agras T25	~20 kg spray / 25 kg spread class	Orchards, vineyards, smaller fields and plots	Compact, foldable frame, orchard-optimized flight modes, RTK compatibility, SmartFarm integration
EAVision (China)	EA-30X	~30 L class (orchards/terraces focused)	Terraced fields, orchards, steep or irregular terrain	AI vision, binocular 3D sensing, automatic terrain-following and height mapping
Hylio (USA)	AG-230	~28 L entry-level tank	Small fields, operators starting with spraying, uneven terrain	Fully made in USA, NDAA-compliant hardware, same software ecosystem as larger Hylio platforms
	AG-272	~38 L tank	Larger U.S. farms and custom applicators needing scalable fleets	Modular design, high-capacity tank, U.S.-built, designed for easy maintenance and fleet expansion
Parrot Drone SAS (France)	Anafi / mapping-focused lines (no spray models)	N/A (no spray tanks)	Mapping, plant health analysis, general ag data collection	GDPR-focused data handling, EU-compliant workflows, "Blue" variants for U.S. DoD and federal use
Rotor Technologies (USA)	Sprayhawk	50 L+ payload	Industrial-scale and mega farms; very large treatment areas	VTOL fixed-wing platform, long-endurance missions, designed for large blocks and long linear runs
XAG (China)	P150	50 kg payload	Industrial-scale row crops, multi-drone ("swarm") fleets	Autonomous swarm operations, high payload, intelligent routing for very large jobs
	P100 Pro	~40 kg payload class	Large operations needing power plus portability	Foldable for transport, RTK-supported precision spraying.
	P40 Pro	Smaller tank (precision-focused)	Smaller fields, high-precision work, obstacle-rich environments	AI-driven precision, dynamic droplet control, RTK GNSS, LiDAR-based obstacle avoidance

<u>Sewer, Pipe & Enclosed Space Inspection</u>

You turn on your spigot and water comes flowing out and down the drain. I'm sure you never think about the magical process involving thousands of miles of underground pipes and pumps, valves and tanks that get it from the source to your home (safely) and back out to the treatment plant down the road. Traditionally, to inspect and repair these sewers and enclosed spaces, workers have had to climb hundreds of feet underground, or waiting for them to fail before digging up streets and roads to find the fault. Ugh. With drones for enclosed spaces, companies and municipalities can inspect and find small issues faster, safer, and before they turn into big problems.

In addition to sewers, companies are taking advantage of this newer class of drones to inspect chemical tanks, mines, nuclear plants, silos, chimneys, and other enclosed spaces, making the job safer while saving thousands of dollars in downtime. With chemical tanks, for instance, the tank has traditionally been emptied, cleaned and scanned for hazardous fumes before inspections could take place. This could take days or weeks and run into the tens of thousands of dollars. A drone with specialized sensors and Lidar capability can fly the job in a day and provide cm-level 3D models pinpointing the exact location of problems. And the mission can be programmed to be repeatable.

Required Equipment

You'll need specialized drones that can fly in GPS-deprived environments on repeatable missions. They must be able to fly with sensors that can detect gas leaks and radiation, map problems, and measure the integrity of metals ultrasonically. They are expensive, but can save thousands of dollars in personnel costs and downtime per job. That means you can charge more for your services.

Industry Trends and Future Outlook

According to <u>Market Research Future</u> and <u>Business Market Insight,</u> the future looks very positive, with a market size estimated to be more than $2.7 billion USD by 2029. Everyone wants to save money and look good to their shareholders, and these drones help them do that. Oh, yeah-they're also safer than traditional methods.

Major Industry Players

Industries include municipalities at the local and state levels, oil and gas suppliers, mining operations, and industrial plants. Think sewers, pipes, tanks, shafts, silos, cooling towers, turbines, chimneys and more. Any company that deals with enclosed spaces, hard-to-reach areas or extreme conditions can probably use these specialized drones to get the work done faster, cheaper, and safer.

How to Break In

The bottom line is that you must have the right drone equipment and be able to operate it. Know your target industries before buying your equipment then pinpoint the best equipment for that industry. Offer flights that demonstrate how easily drones can save money quickly and be ready to back it up with facts and figures. If you're not an expert in the field, study up or partner with someone who is. This person may also have contacts that can jumpstart your marketing and sales efforts.

What You Can Charge

For flying enclosed spaces and GPS-denied environments, you can charge a premium depending on the service and equipment needed for the job. For sewers and pipes, you could easily start at $3,000.00 per job and go up from there. For tanks and hazardous conditions, the range could be $5,000-$10,000 per job depending on the necessary sensors and the technical skill and software needed to capture and analyze the data. You'll need to base your rates on which drone and sensors you're using, any extra personnel you have to hire, and the amount of post-flight processing you have to do.

Drones and What They Cost

The leader in this field is **Flyability** with its' *Elios* 3 drone. This one can fly a number of payloads for just about any enclosed space operation. And while a quick internet search will bring up the "Skydio R10" as a cheaper option, it depends on your end use. The R10 seems to be more for quick deployment and "tactical entry". Choosing between the two depends on whether your priority is live video and communication for operational awareness (R10) or high-fidelity 3D surveys and high-quality inspection data (Elios 3).

Comparing the Flyability Elios 3 and the Skydio R10.

Aspect	Elios 3	Skydio R10
Primary Use	Detailed 3D mapping and surveying of confined spaces (tunnels, sewers, tanks, etc).	Tactical, indoor inspections, situational awareness in tight & confined spaces.
Navigation	SLAM with LiDAR (no GPS/compass), real-time 3D mapping.	AI-driven obstacle avoidance with stereo cameras, Sensors for zero-light.
Lighting and Visibility	Uses sensors including visible, thermal, and LiDAR.	Built-in LED floodlights for dark environments.
Payload Options	Modular sensors for photogrammetry, thermal, LiDAR surveying.	Media-focused (audio/video), livestreaming capabilities.
Data Output	High-precision 3D maps and point clouds for analysis.	Live video, audio, and situational data.
Durability	Collision/impact resistant design.	Propeller guards, low-cost to repair.
Flight Duration and Coverage	Mapping up to 300 meters in tunnels per flight.	Designed for quick deployment and navigation in tight spaces.
Typical Usage Environments	Underground vaults, tunnels, confined spaces for industrial inspection.	Indoor, tactical entries, close quarter patrol, GPS-denied environments.

The cool thing about the Elios 3 is that it uses "SLAM" navigation (Simultaneous Localization and Mapping) to build a map of its' unknown environment while simultaneously tracking its own position within it. Using special algorithms, SLAM brings together sensor data from LiDAR, RGB cameras, and the drone's IMU to create the real-time 2D or 3D map. It identifies features to use as reference points, predicts motion, and corrects errors as it flies. This makes it perfect for GPS-denied environments like underground tunnels and mines.

A Look Ahead

Coming up in the next chapter, we'll take an updated look at some industries where drones have been working for quite some time, and what it takes for you to make it as a service provider in each of these areas.

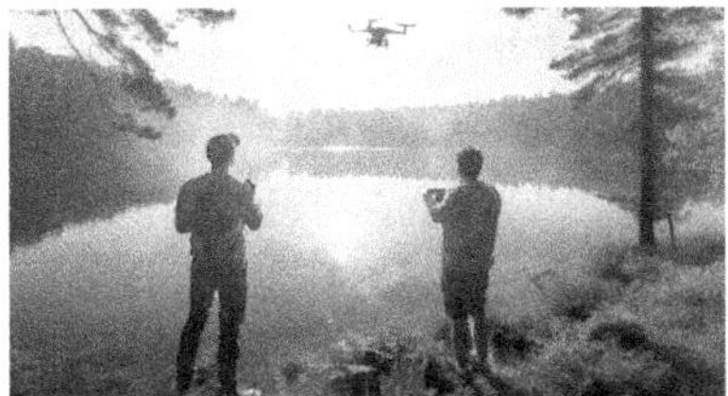

> "The moment you doubt whether you can fly,
> you cease for ever to be able to do it."
> —J.M. Barrie in "Peter Pan"

L et's look at some traditional industries that use drones, and what it takes to get started in each. Drone pilots have been earning money in these areas for quite some time. These are in addition to the "emerging industries" outlined in the previous chapter with some overlap in the energy sector.

Selling Stock Footage

How much you can make: $5-$150+ for stills; $10-$400+ for video.

Special Skills: Drone License (FAA or EAA Certification).

Minimum Drone Capabilities: 4K video and 20mp still photos, Raw (DNG) record capability; 3-axis gimbal stabilization.

Drones in this Category: Phantom 4 Pro (No longer in production), DJI Air 2S, Air 3, Mini 3 & 4 Pro, Autel Evo Nano+, Others.

How to get the work: Of all the categories, I consider this one to be the easiest to break into. Nevertheless, before you actually sell something, *you must objectively assess your abilities and your library of stock footage.* Look at stock libraries and the footage they're offering. Ask yourself how the quality and variety of shots in your personal library stacks up to other drone footage on the market. How many different shots do you have of each subject? Do you own the rights to the footage? (If not, you cannot sell it). Has it been used or sold somewhere else? If so, you can only sell it if you have a "non-exclusive" usage contract with the first client you've sold it to or flown it for. Ask others for an objective assessment of your shots.

Your Approach

There are two basic ways of selling and licensing still photos and footage: "Non-Exclusive" or "Exclusive". With *non-exclusive* licensing, any client who hires you gets access to the footage and/or still images to use, but you retain the right to sell and/or license them to others as well. You make less, but you are selling it to multiple customers. On the other hand, If the client prefers an *exclusive* license, you can charge significantly more for that. With an exclusive license, the customer is buying the sole rights to the photo or video. Nobody else can use it, and you cannot sell or license it to any other entity. Keep this in mind when executing contracts with your regular drone clients. If you can keep non-exclusive rights (granting your customer non-exclusive rights, as well), you can resell that same footage as stock footage to other entities.

Some highly successful drone ops spend their spare time shooting specifically for the stock footage market. They identify popular subjects, go out and fly/record them and list them with stock footage sites. This is called speculation or "spec" work because you don't get paid unless the photo or video sells. If you have the time and inclination, you can sell the stock footage yourself on your own website. The upside is that you keep 100% of the profits, but it's time-consuming, especially to get up and running. With this method, you'll be designing a web presence and having to devise some sort of marketing scheme to drive customers to your site. Then, you'll need a way for them to pay and download the shot securely. It's quite involved, and the backend selling part can become expensive to set up and maintain. The preferred method for me is to sell through established stock footage sites. Decide if you want to target drone-only sites or allow it to be featured everywhere. Depending on the site, you may want an exclusive contract with the vendor.

Keep these tips in mind when shooting for the stock footage market:

1. Shoot the highest quality possible: Raw for stills and 4K or higher for Video.
2. Include both processed (Color graded) and unprocessed photos of the same image.
3. Don't sign exclusivity contracts unless they pay higher percentages.
4. Include something in the shot for scale when shooting wide shots.
5. Always try to capture the shot with and without people.
6. Get releases for any identifiable people in the shot and locations. Check with each footage site you intend to work with as they will each have their own policies on releases and may have specific forms to use.
7. Make sure you have the right to fly and capture images. Illegally-obtained footage may not be marketable and could get you in trouble.
8. Capture your subject at all times of the day. This gives you a greater variety of shots without moving from site to site.
9. Include foreground objects to add a dynamic element to the shot.
10. Capture hyperlapses with moving elements to add interest to the shot.
11. Catalog your footage as soon as possible while the mission is fresh in your mind. Be sure to note any specifics of the location and subject in case you're asked.

When looking at companies to work with, see if they have any special features for submitters. For instance, "Shutterstock" has something they call "The Shot List" that tells you the most requested content on the site to gauge what's selling and what's not.

Here's a non-exhaustive list of "Entry Level" drones that would work for stock footage and still images.

Drone	Quality	Price (USD)	Notable Features
Autel EVO Lite+	20 MP 4K-6K	$900+	Variable aperture, RAW stills, long flight time.
Autel EVO Nano+	50 MP 4K 30fps	$700	Vibrant color, compact, great for low light.
DJI Air 3	20 MP 4K/5K	$1,200	Dual camera, obstacle avoidance, RAW photos.
DJI Mini 3 Pro	48 MP/ 4K 60fps	$750	Lightweight, RAW photos, good beginner drone.
DJI Mini 4 Pro	48 MP 4K/100fps	$800	RAW stills, HDR video, compact, obstacle avoidance.
DJI Mini 5 Pro	50 MP 4K/120fps	$999	RAW photos, AI tracking.
Holy Stone HS710E	20 MP 4K/30fps	~$230	Affordable, beginner-friendly, voice control.
Potensic Atom SE	20 MP 4K/30fps	~$280	Budget option, GPS-assisted stability.

This is just an example of what is available. Remember that in the U.S., many foreign-made drones and parts are now being treated as "national security risks". It **does not ban existing models** authorized before December 22, 2025. But, if you're looking for approved drones made in the United States, you're going to pay a lot more at this level. In addition, most entry-level drones don't have variable shutter speeds which is key for quality video capture. The takeaway? Do your homework, know your needs and put as much money towards your primary drone as you possibly can. You'll be glad you did in the long run.

Category 2: Aerial Cinematography

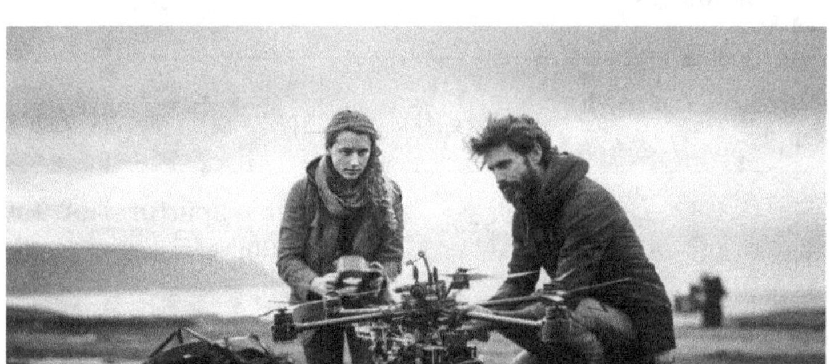

How much you can make: $50-500/hour or more.

Special Skills: 30 hours or more of flight time (300 hours or more preferred for high-end jobs); photography/videography skills helpful, experience flying around moving vehicles and actors; knowledge of and experience working on and around film and video sets. Some productions may require the camera person to be in the union. If that is the case, you'll have to join the union or find an operator to work with you who is a union member.

Minimum Drone capabilities:

- 4K video (3840 x 2160) & 20mp still photos;

- Raw (DNG) Photo record capability;

- ProRes and RAW video record capability suggested;

- 3-Axis Gimbal with 360-degree movement capability;

- Dual control-capable drone preferred (Pilot/Camera Operator).

These are the *minimum* drone capabilities for cinematography. Many feature film and some broadcast TV projects will require a drone with detachable cameras and lenses that can record up to 8K. For corporate video, independent films and streaming, 4K with ProRes capabilities may be enough.

Drones in the 8K category: (DJI): Matrice Series, Inspire 3; Mavic 4 Pro, (Autel): EVO II Pro; (Freefly): Alta, Astro; (Sony): Airpeak S1; (Watts Innovations): Prism Sky. (These are examples; there are others).

Drones in the 4-6K category: (DJI): Inspire 2, Mavic 3 Pro Cine, (Autel): EVO II 8k, EVO Lite+; others.

Who hires you: Film and video production companies, Directors, Producers, Production Coordinators, Art Directors.

How to get work: This is the glamor category with potentially big budgets and lots of high-pressure flights. Missions can range from simple shot lists the client provides (that you fly and capture alone) to multi-million-dollar movie sets with many moving parts. This category requires experience and knowledge. Experience flying, of course, but also the knowledge that comes with it. Knowledge about lighting, camera settings, shot composition, and movement best suited for a drone.

With Aerial Cinematography, if you're halfway decent, you can start with small jobs and potentially work your way up to big-budget, high-paying gigs, but not overnight. The entry point for feature films is high and very competitive, with less than a handful of operators regularly getting the nod to work on set. To get to the top here, you've got to pay your dues, learn the craft, and eventually invest in high-dollar drones and ancillary gear. Even then, it's not guaranteed.

If you're a visual person with an eye for composition and lighting, this could be a highly enjoyable process, even if you decide Hollywood isn't for you. Basic shot techniques and movements apply to every aspect of the industry, whether you're flying b-roll for a local production company or chase scenes for a potential blockbuster movie. And, if you're an established videographer or photographer, you can easily add drones to your toolbox and upsell your value to the client. If not, partner with one. Work with independents; post your work online.

Find a niche and fill it. In the Washington, DC area where I fly, competition is tough, especially for aerial cinematography. In addition, the airspace is the most highly regulated in the country, but flyable if you know the procedures for authorizations and waivers necessary to launch here. I have been flying the airspace since the restrictions were put in place. It's one of the niches I've identified and filled to my advantage. Find your niche and set yourself apart.

See examples of classic drone shots: www.MikeSobola.com/resources.

Here is a chart comparing cinema-quality drones.

Drone	Camera / Mount Type	Max Video Res. & Codecs (Typical)	Price (USD)	Notes
Autel EVO II Pro (6K) (China)	Integrated 1″ gimbal camera.	Up to 6K/30 & 4K/60 in H.264/H.265 (no internal ProRes).	$2,500.00	Strong image quality for mid-tier professional work where ProRes is not required.
Freefly Alta X (USA)	Heavy-lift platform for cinema cameras.	Depends on camera (Alexa Mini/LF/35, RED, Venice 2, etc.).	$20K-$25K	Top-tier heavy-lift for major film sets needing full-size cine bodies and lenses.
Freefly Astro (USA)	Standard 61 MP Sony payload options (mapping/cine).	High-res stills and up to 6K-class video (H.264/H.265).	$20K-$26K	Mid-sized platform for high-res imaging, mapping, and lighter-weight cine work.
Sony Airpeak S1 (Japan)	Gimbal platform for Alpha/FX3 series.	Matches attached Sony body (4K/6K/8K) including XAVC / RAW via camera.	$11K + Lenses & Accessories	Discontinued 2025, but supported until 2030.
Watts Innov. PRISM Sky (USA)	Heavy-lift, open-architecture NDAA-compliant platform	Determined by payload: supports cinema cameras and specialty payloads	$26K-$30K	Versatile, made-in-USA heavy-lift for productions needing NDAA compliance and modular workflows.
Arc Sky/ X55 (USA)	Phase One P3 or Sony ILX-LR1	Depends on camera; supports cinema workflows.	$40,000-$50,000	Designed for high-res aerial inspection, mapping, and surveying; video capable.
DJI Inspire 3 (China)	Zenmuse X9 -8K Air gimbal camera.	Up to 8K ProRes RAW / Cinema DNG, multiple ProRes 422 variants.	$17,000	Flagship integrated cinema drone for narrative, commercials, and high-end TV work.
DJI Mavic 3 Pro Cine	Integrated triple-camera gimbal (Hasselblad wide +2 tele lenses).	Up to 5.1K or 4K high-bitrate, ProRes 422 variants, 1 TB internal SSD.	$5,000	Compact "all-in-one" ProRes platform for run-and-gun, travel, and B-cam aerials.
DJI Mavic 4	Triple-camera system and longer endurance.	6K/60p HDR and high-frame-rate 4K, plus 10-bit profiles, and larger gimbal tilt than previous versions.	$4,500	No ProRes, but comparable All-I encoding (lacks ProRes compatibility in some editing systems w/o transcoding.)

This category also has a much larger selection of drones made in the United States due to the higher price point for most of the aircraft.

Category 3: Construction Imaging

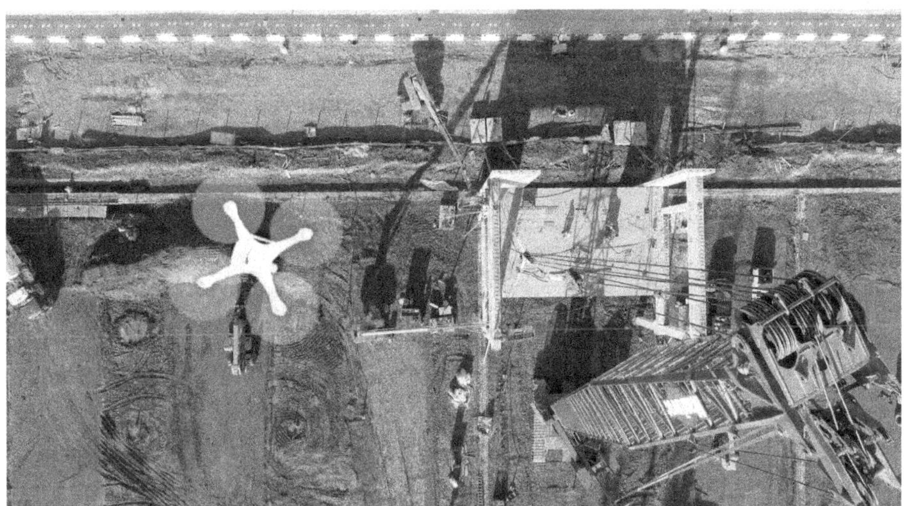

How much you can make: $25-$100 per hour.

Special Skills: Mapping software use, Acquisition for 3D modeling, Ground Control Point theory and utilization (preferred), basic video editing.

Minimum Drone capabilities: 4K video (3840 x 2160) and 12 mp still photos (20 MP preferred); Mechanical Shutter; 3-Axis Gimbal (pitch/roll/yaw).

Drones in this category: DJI Matrice Series, DJI Phantom 4 Pro, DJI Inspire Series, DJI Mavic 3E, Autel EVO II Pro 6K Enterprise, Wingtra One Gen II / Wingtra RAY, Quantum Trinity Pro, Freefly Astro, Skyfish, others.

Who hires you: Building owners, construction companies (Project Managers and Digital Asset Managers).

How to Get Work: Construction rework costs typically range from 5-12% of total project budgets, equating to billions annually in wasted funds across the industry. Drone imaging can save money by spotting problems early and preventing "rework". It can also speed pre-construction site work and preparation, document safety compliance, and allow a deeper visibility into the site on a regular basis.

Talk to the Project Manager on a construction site. Set up meetings with the Digital Asset Manager of a construction company. Find building owners of new construction as it's breaking ground. If possible, fly the site when it's closed and process an orthomosaic map before any meeting. Show them what drone imaging can deliver and offer an introductory flight for free.

How a Drone Fits Into the Picture

Here's an example of what can be done with an orthomosaic from standard drone images: https://youtu.be/sCcGKJ4NdjU. Using a regular, out-of-the-box drone and mapping software (such as "Drone Deploy" or "Pix 4D") you can automate flights to capture site photos, and stitch them into a high-resolution Orthomosaic "map" of the site. This map can be used to calculate volumes of dirt piles and stock piles onsite and take accurate measurements for material ordering. Drone data and images can also be used to produce contour maps (or "topos") and "plan overlays". This is where the architectural plan is aligned over the drone map to check accuracy of the site compared to the plan and placement of utilities, walls, drainage ponds and more.

Topographic maps and overlays require specific precision to align the drone data with the global grid. The drone gets this precision by using surveyed points or "Ground Control Points" which correct for inaccuracies in height and position. Ground control points and drone flight accuracy is beyond the scope of this book, but can be explored further through one of the training programs mentioned at www.MikeSobola.com/resources.

Construction imaging is a good base to build on since projects are usually weekly or bi-weekly for 12-18 months at a time. While the rate per-mission can be lower than one-offs, the frequency and duration of the contracts usually makes up for it in the form of steady income. Standard deliverables include things such as Orthomosaic Maps (https://youtu.be/KrjQy3BkWPw), Progress Photos, and Edited Videos (https://youtu.be/YaIuiEIn9fY). Non-standard items such as Topographic maps, plan overlays and 3D models are usually an extra charge and provided on an as-needed basis.

Let's compare a few construction-focused drones.

Drone	Manuf. Country	Price (USD)	Key Features	Drawbacks
DJI Matrice 350 RTK	China	$11K–$15K	55-min flight, 45MP full-frame P1 camera, cm RTK, IP55, LiDAR op.	High payload costs, DJI software lock-in.
DJI Mavic 3E	China	$4K–$6K	45-min, 20MP mech. shutter, cm RTK, portable.	Smaller sensor, low-light limits.
Freefly Alta X	USA/ Mixed	$15K–$25K	RTK, Heavy Phase One/Sony payloads.	15–20 min battery, heavy, manual piloting.
SenseFly eBee X	Switz.	$15K–$25K	90-min fixed-wing, PPK/RTK 1–3cm accuracy, high-res cameras.	Fragile terrain, long setup time.
SmartDrone Magellan	USA	$55K	LiDAR/photo., civil eng-focused.	Needs ground station for accuracy; only 12mp stills.
WingtraOne Gen II	Switz.	$25K–$35K	59-min VTOL, PPK 1–3cm accuracy, 42MP Sony RX1R II, 100s acres/ flight, fixed wing.	VLOS-limited, large-scale sites only.
WISPR Ranger Pro	USA	$20K–$30K	NDAA, LiDAR, photogrammetry, rugged, georef. point clouds.	Limited specs, enterprise pricing.
WISPR SkyScout	USA	$20K–$30K	Sub-cm survey grade, RTK or PPK available.	Limited specs, enterprise pricing.

Category 4: Thermal Imaging & Inspection

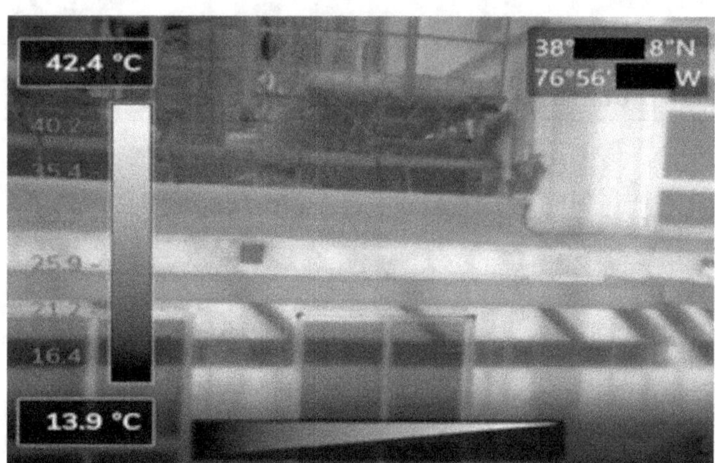

How much you can make: $50-$500/hour

Special Skills: Thermal Imaging Experience. For radiometric cameras, a Level 1 Thermography certification is preferred.

Minimum Drone capabilities: (RGB Camera): 4K video (3840 x 2160) and 20mp still photos; (Thermal Camera): 320 x 240 or 640 x 512 (Preferred); 3-Axis Gimbal (pitch/roll/yaw); 3-way obstacle avoidance.

Drones in this Category: DJI Matrice 350 RTK, Autel EVO Max 4T, DJI Mavic 3T, Teledyne FLIR SIRAS (Discontinued, but still available), Skydio X10, AceCore Zoe, DraganFly Commander 3XL, others.

Who hires you: Insurance companies, Builders, Homeowners, General Contractors.

How to get work: Contact builders, construction contractors, insurance companies and roofing companies to offer your services. Using relatively inexpensive (non-radiometric) systems, thermal imaging with a drone is safer and quicker than sending a worker up on a ladder to walk a roof or scan a problem spot in a building envelope. Remember that unless you also have an RGB camera mounted, your images will be infrared and subject to interpretation.

Sensors

There are two types of Infrared or IR sensors: Radiometric and non-radiometric. Non-radiometric cameras are inexpensive and easy to use, simply displaying differences in temperature where the camera is pointed. They take no specialized training to interpret, but you do need software to make sense of the data and present it to the client. On the other hand, Radiometric cameras measure precise temperature differences and must be calibrated. You should have a thermal certification to properly and effectively calibrate the sensor and to utilize and interpret the data from a radiometric camera. Radiometric cameras can cost as much as $10,000 or more.

Popular software for analyzing and presenting thermal data and images is listed on the accompanying page of my website at www.MikeSobola.com/resources. Thermal imaging is a good tool to have in your drone capabilities toolbox, but you probably can't rely on it as your main source of income due to the infrequent use you'll see for the specialized camera and drone. If possible, buy a drone that has the IR capabilities and RGB (visual) camera as well, so that you can make money with more conventional done jobs and then supplement these with the thermal capabilities when the client requests them.

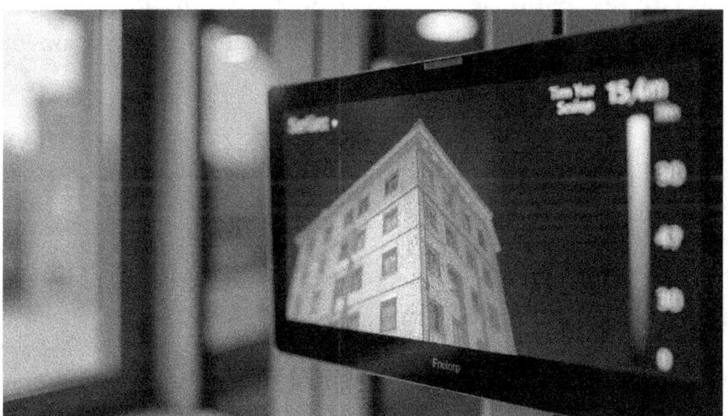

Thermal imaging can add value to your drone services.

Category 5: Aerial Inspection (Solar Panels, Power Lines, Cell Towers, Wind Turbines).

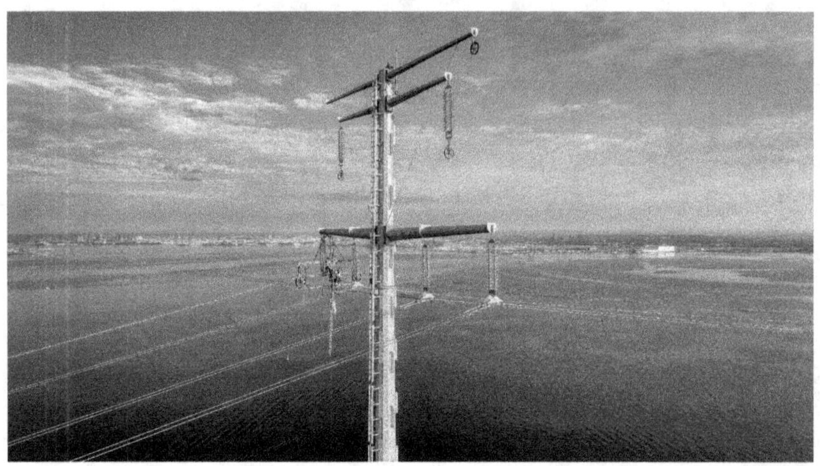

How much you can make: $50-100 per hour. Most pay a flat rate per item inspected.

Special Skills: 3D Mapping experience preferred. Thermal experience required for solar panels, BVLOS waiver for pipeline and powerlines.

Minimum Drone capabilities: 4K video (3840 x 2160) and 20mp still photos, Zoom capability preferred, (Solar Panels): 320 x 240 Thermal Camera, 3-Axis Gimbal (pitch/roll/yaw), 3-way obstacle avoidance.

Drones in this category: DJI Matrice 350 RTK, DKI Mavic 3 E, Skydio X10, Watts Innovations Prism Sky, Parrot Anafi USA, Autel Evo Max 4T, Freefly Alta X, Voliro T, others.

Who hires you: Builders, solar installation companies, cell tower owners, inspection companies and window companies.

How you get the work: Cell tower inspections are normally contracted out in mass by the tower owners. The inspection company then hires you (the drone pilot) on a per-tower basis. Specifications are rigorous and the risk is on the drone pilot - you don't get paid unless you fly the tower and deliver the specific data as outlined by the client. Towers are normally in sparsely-populated and remote locations meaning your travel time between sites can be extensive. We cover more details in the previous chapter on "Emerging Areas for Drones".

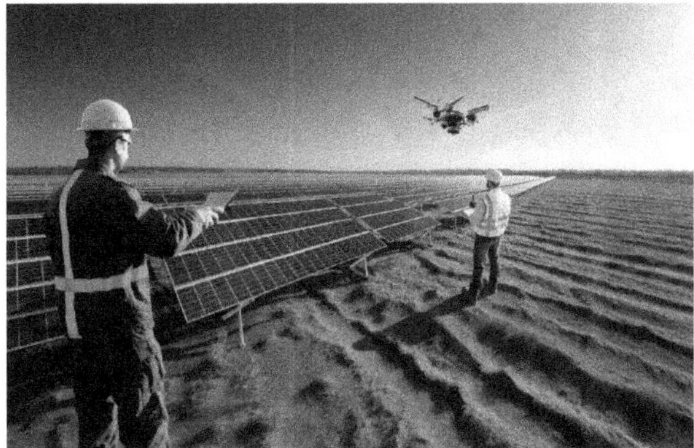

Solar inspections via thermal imaging is a different animal. You must be able to fly a pre-programmed "map" of the solar farm and correlate that with a visual map of the panels in order to enable quick location of problem panels. Depending on the client deliverable needs, radiometric or non-radiometric thermal cameras can be used. Your insurance requirements (the amount you should carry) for solar inspections is normally much higher than other industries owing to the amount of damage that can easily be done from a drone crashing into the panels and the cost of replacing any damaged drones due to drone failure and crashing.

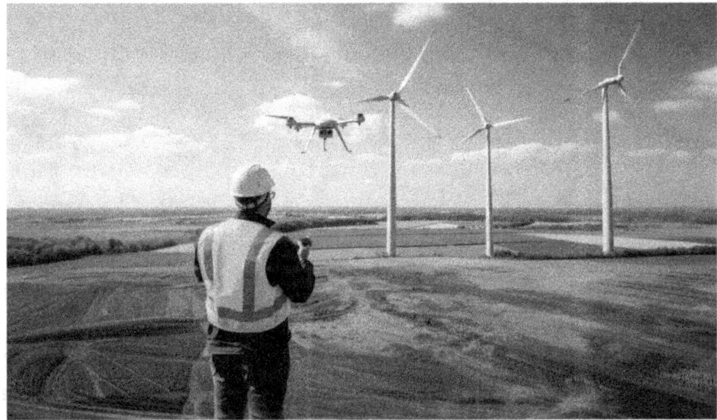

For **wind turbines,** some clients ask for high-resolution pictures, others want 3D models of the propeller area. In either case, it pays to have a drone with high-quality zoom capabilities or a telephoto lens in order to maintain a safe distance from the wind turbine. You're usually looking for frayed wires, loose or rusted parts or damage caused by flying objects and weather events. In most cases, specific coordination is needed to ensure that the turbines are not moving while the inspection is taking place.

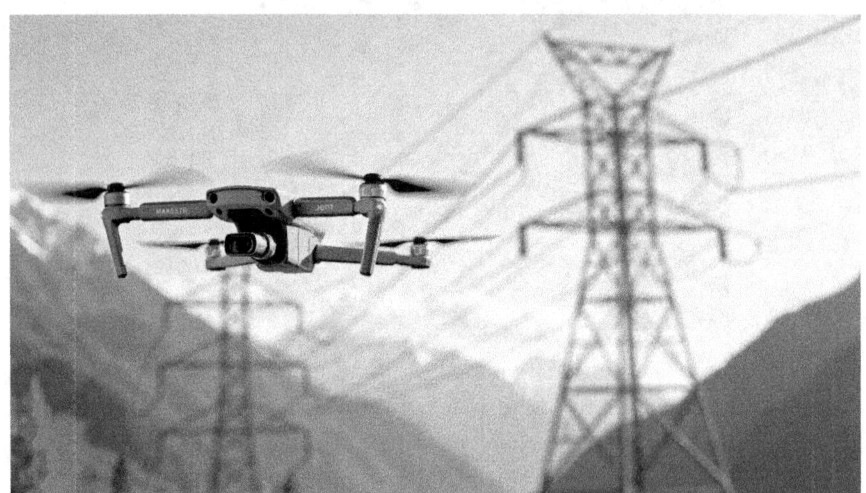

Power line inspection takes special drones

For **power lines and gas lines**, most inspections are done with in-house drone operators and aircraft due to the high cost of the specialized equipment required. For gas line inspection alone, the sensor can run upwards of $100,000.00. In addition, large companies file for Beyond Visual Line of Sight or "BVLOS" Waivers in order to effectively and economically inspect long tracts of power lines and pipelines that can run for hundreds of miles. BVLOS waivers are difficult and expensive for individuals to obtain and make power line and pipeline inspection uneconomical for the freelance drone pilot unless you have an established relationship with the client.

For high tension power lines, a shielded drone may also be required which drives up the initial cost of entry to this market. The upside is that many companies have training programs with specialized equipment to teach drone pilots both staff and freelance) how to fly power lines safely and effectively. Going through one of these training programs is highly beneficial if you can get enrolled. Just know that this area is highly-specialized and like other similar areas, it helps to have a background in the power like industry or to partner with someone who does.

Category 6: Commercial Real Estate

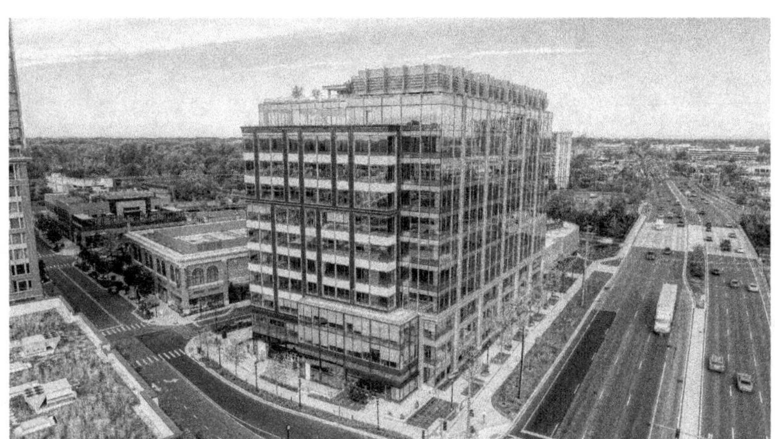

How much you can make: $500-$2,500 and up per site.

Special Skills: Aerial Cinematography.

Minimum Drone capabilities: 4K video (3840 x 2160) and 20mp still photos, Raw (DNG).

Drones in this category: DJI Phantom 4 Series, DJI Mavic Series, DJI Mini 3 Pro, Mini 4, Pro, Mini 5 Pro, DJI Air 2S, DJI Air 3, Syma X-500, Autel EVO Nano+, Freefly Alta Series, Yuneec H520, Others.

Who hires you: Real Estate Agents, Developers, REIT property holders.

How to get work: Attach yourself to a still photographer and production company. Give discounts for "sole provider" status where your contact (agent or company) calls you for all their drone imaging needs exclusively). Put together demo reels and target them online with LinkedIn and Twitter. Have a YouTube and Vimeo Channel. This category relies on aerial cinematography skills to know the most effective video moves and best photo angles and lighting tricks in order to get the best shots possible. Pick a building and scout the location three times a day: early morning, late afternoon and at sunset to see how different lighting conditions affect your shots of the property. Fly buildings that may be up for sale or lease and offer the images to the real estate agent in return for credit and referrals (and the chance at future work with the agency). Having images of the actual property (not just a similar one) can quickly close the sale and earn you a longtime client down the road.

Category 7: Residential Real Estate

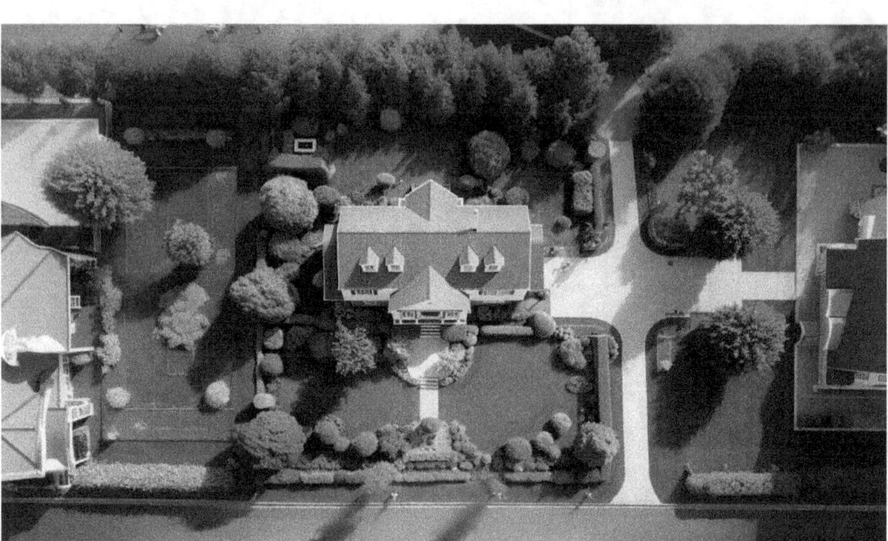

How much you can make: $25-$1,000 per property.

Special Skills: Aerial Cinematography.

Minimum Drone capabilities: 4K video (3840 x 2160) and 20mp still photos, Raw (DNG) Photo record capability, 3-Axis Gimbal.

Drones in this category: DJI Phantom 4 Series, DJI Mavic Series, DJI Mini 3 Pro, Mini 4, Pro, Mini 5 Pro, DJI Air 2S, DJI Air 3, Syma X-500, Autel EVO Nano+, Freefly Alta Series, Yuneec H520, Others.

Who hires you: Realtors or homeowners looking to showcase a property for sale, real estate photographers.

How to get work: Residential real estate is normally best left for the side gig. Many realtors or associates fly themselves and capture their own images. When they do hire pilots, the pay is usually on the low end of the pay scale. The exception is for very high-end luxury properties. Find these high-dollar realtors and offer your exclusive service to them, but be prepared to add interior shots with the drone and a traditional camera package and to knock their socks off with a demo reel. Team up with photographers to add value to their traditional services. As with commercial real estate, aerial cinematography skills are required as is an understanding of lighting and camera angles & moves.

Category 8: Search & Rescue (SAR)

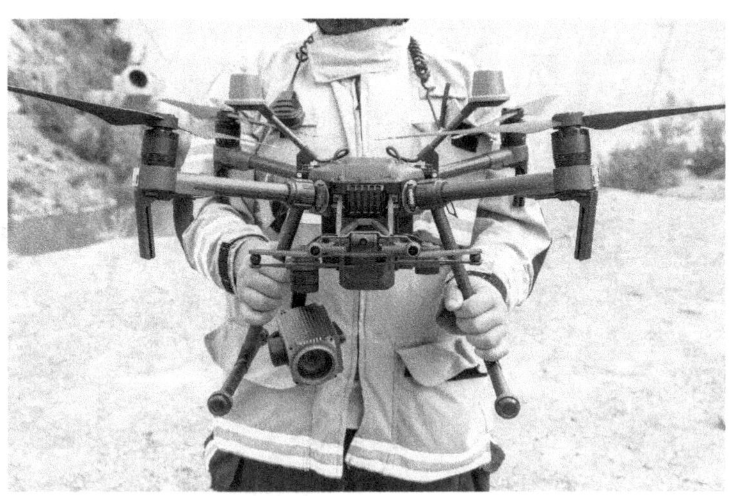

How much you can make: $40,000-$65,000 per year (staff) or $20-$80 per hour (Independent).

Special Skills: Thermal Imaging, SAR training.

Minimum Drone capabilities: 4K video (3840 x 2160) and 20mp still photos, Zoom lens capable of 30x or greater, Thermal sensor (with RGB overlay preferred), 3-Axis Gimbal (pitch/roll/yaw), 3-way obstacle avoidance.

Drones that fit this category: Acecore Zoe, Autel EVO Max 4T, BRINC Lemur 2, Draganfly Commander 3XL, DJI Matrice 30T/350 RTK, DJI Mavic 3T, Parrot Anafi USA, Skydio X10, others.

Who hires you: Search and Rescue professionals normally have internal resources for including drones in their rescue operations. When outside drone help is recruited, it is many times on a volunteer basis to smaller SAR operations (such as volunteer fire departments and rescue squads).

How to get work: Contact SAR outfits in your town and offer your services. Local municipalities often don't have the budget for their own departments, so they hire out or rely on state resources. Reach out to local fire and rescue companies with your capabilities. Put together a short video demo on what drone SAR looks like and what your equipment can do.

Category 9: Weddings & Events

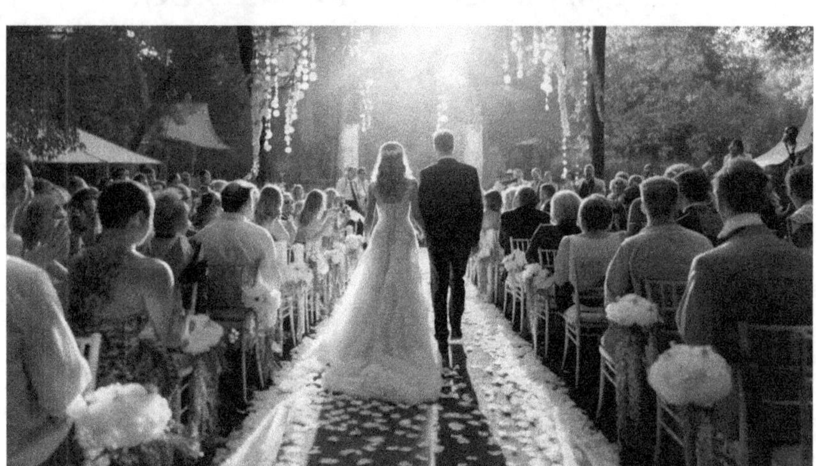

How much you can make: $50-300 per hour depending on event.

Special Skills: Organizational skills, able to pivot and think quickly.

Minimum Drone capabilities:, 4K video (3840 x 2160) and 20mp still photos, Raw (DNG) Photo record capability, 3-Axis Gimbal (pitch/roll/yaw), 3-way obstacle avoidance.

Drones in this category: DJI Mini 3 Pro, Mini 4 Pro, Mini 5 Pro, DJI Air 2S, Syma X-500, Autel Robotics EVO Nano+, Others.

Who hires you: Brides, Event Planners, Wedding Planners, Event Rental Facilities, Photographers, Videographers, Event facilities.

How to Get Work: Find event planners and offer them a free marketing reel in exchange for client referrals. Offer discounts and referral fees. Attach yourself to a photographer who is already working weddings and events. This industry is a high-stress environment with lots of competition. Drone shots are normally a small part of a larger overall photo and video package, so this is best worked as an upsell for established photographers and videographers who want to add drones to their event packages. Partnering with the pros who want to offer drone imaging, but don't fly is a foot in the door, but be sure to negotiate a payment package that works for you since it's the photographer's contract.

Category 10: Urban Planning

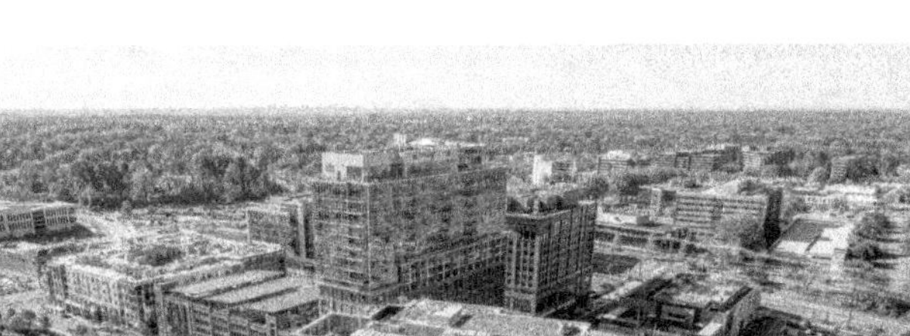

How much you can make: $25-100 per hour (Normally bid by the job).

Special Skills: Mapping and Photogrammetry software experience, Aerial Cinematography.

Minimum Drone capabilities:, 4K video (3840 x 2160) and 20mp still photos, Raw (DNG) Photo record capability, 3-Axis Gimbal (pitch/roll/yaw.

Drones in this category: DJI Mavic Series, DJI Mini 3 Pro, Mini 4 pro, Mini 5 Pro, DJI Air 2S, DJI Air 3, Syma X-500, Autel Robotics EVO Nano+, Others.

Who hires you: Municipalities and state government entities, parks commissions, planning commissions, state and municipal road departments.

How to get work: Contact state and local governments, parks commissions, and roads/maintenance departments. Look for municipalities with high-income demographics and target the parks departments first. County parks departments with large marketing budgets are good candidates for showcasing venue events in their parks as well as the parks themselves. Offer Orthomosaic maps of the parks that show facility, foliage and landscape conditions. Present a demo on how your drone can aid in everything from landscape and tree inspection to building façade, road and facility inspection; saving time and money along the way. Your high-resolution Orthomosaic "map" is like a current Google map of their park or facility that is up to date and higher resolution. Buildings can be modeled in 3D to show problems and urban plans can be supplemented by up-to-date imaging to show current traffic pattern flow, bottlenecks, and canopy coverage over specific areas.

Category 11: Agricultural/Landscape Analysis

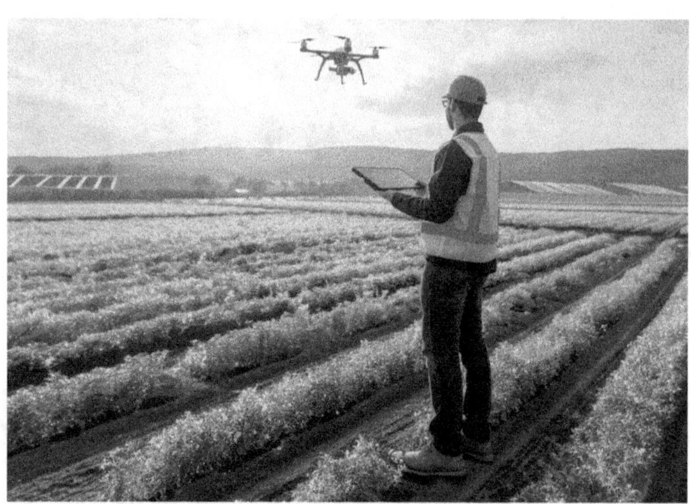

How much you can make: $25-400 per hour.

Special Skills: Photogrammetry and Mapping, Topographical Map Generation, Knowledge of Agriculture analytical software.

Minimum Drone capabilities: 4K video (3840 x 2160) and 20mp still photos, 3-Axis Gimbal (pitch/roll/yaw), 3-way obstacle avoidance, Multi-spectral camera (for turf analysis).

Drones in this category: DJI Mavic 3M, AgEagle eBee Ag, DJI Matrice 350 RTK, Yuneec H520 RTK, Parrot Bluegrass Fields (older, but still available), Wingtra One, EVO Max 4T, Others.

Who hires you: Golf courses, high-end landscaping companies, farmers.

How to get work: Contact facility managers at high-end private golf courses and demonstrate what you can do. Offer a free turf analysis and interpretation. The cost of multispectral sensors drives up the cost of entry to this industry as a drone service provider. In addition, due to the slim margins involved, many farmers run their own drone programs and have access to free analysis services from seed and fertilizer companies. Golf course marketing with turf analysis and topographical maps is good, but requires vertical accuracy, so ground control points or an RTK drone with real time correction is required (and expensive).

This is not an exhaustive list, obviously. The key is to find an industry that you feel comfortable servicing, that is well-represented in your area in terms of the number of jobs taking place, and to define your niche within those industries that you do choose to serve so that you can set yourself apart from the competition.

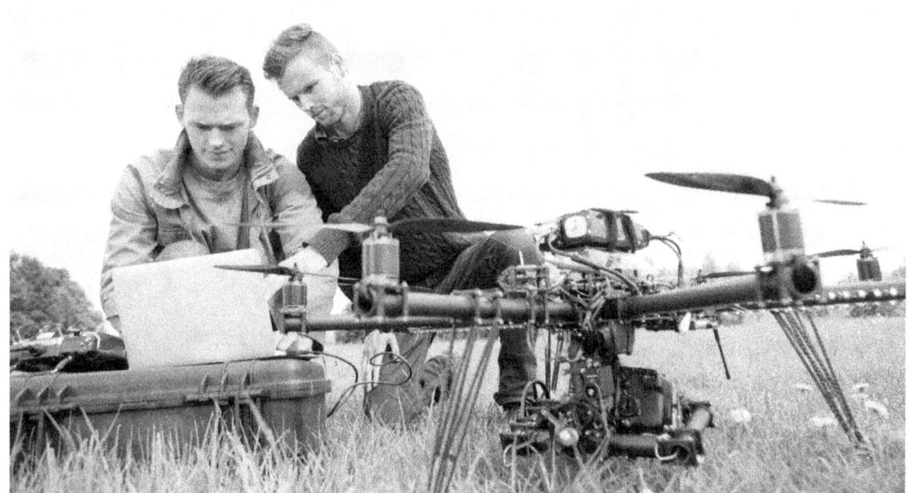

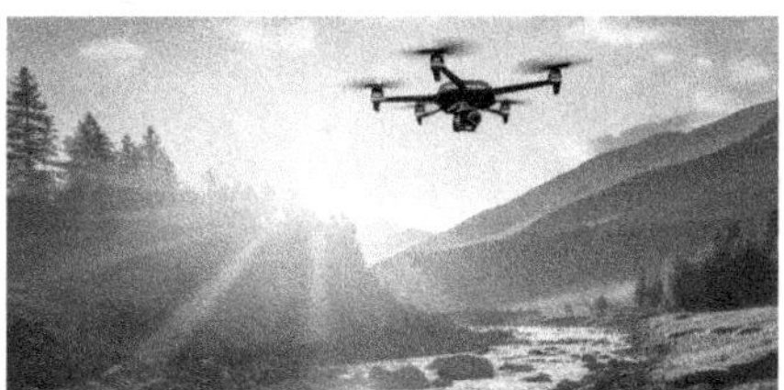

Chapter 12:
Parting Words

Always remember that your drone is a tool. To be successful in finding customers and growing your business, you've got to demonstrate how it can benefit *the client's business*. Do your research, find out what's important to them and how you can add value with your drone imaging. It's key to define your niche within those industries that you do choose to serve so that you can set yourself apart from the competition. What do you do better? What cna you do differently? Is there a new drone application that you can provide that will be useful to your customer that nobody else has thought of?

Our industry is evolving quickly. It's important to stay on top of changes in regulations and technology in order to stay relevant and legal. Ultimately, you are in the business of finding a solution to your clients' problems. Know your craft inside out by taking online courses and flying every day. Learn from others and don't be afraid to ask questions and offer advice. Watch other drone videos from successful pilots in your industries. Adapt their techniques to your workflow. Learn from different conditions and environments and then share what you learn.

Become a thought leader. Reach out on social media and become part of the community. Be honest in your abilities and judge your own work clearly. If you apply yourself and you're always trying to improve, you'll separate yourself from others. And, before you know it, you'll have new pilots asking advice and to work as *your* Visual Observer.

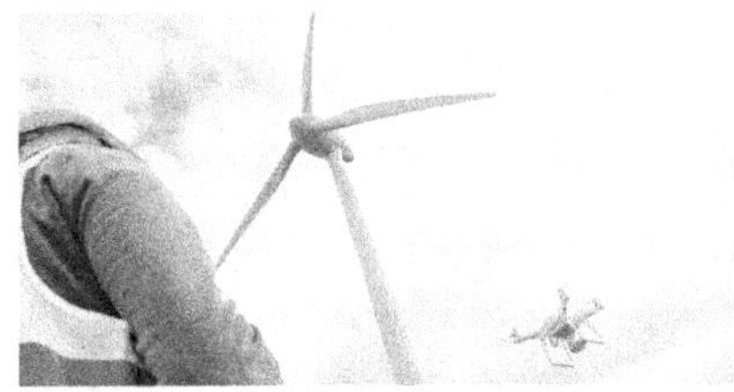

15-Day Action Plan

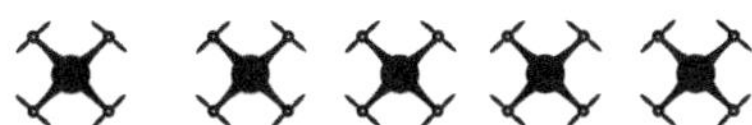

A daily step-by-step guide to jump start cash flow in your new business. This plan assumes that you have taken and passed your applicable drone exam and have the necessary certifications to fly recreationally or commercially.

Day 1: Company Tools and Identity. Research and buy your drone. Devise a company name and brainstorm your logo. Find a designer for your logo and web site. Start on your website design. Using the information from chapter 8, pinpoint your target industries. Talk to other pilots in your selected industries and read reviews for the applicable drones. Select and purchase your drone based on current and projected future needs. Be sure to include extra batteries, memory cards and filters. Use the information from the "Resources" section to begin your logo and web site design. Start by making a list of other web sites that you like and why you like them. Sketch out a sitemap of how you want your website to flow.

Day 2: Drone Set-up, Logo Work & Website Design. Read the manual that comes with the drone. Watch an unboxing video on YouTube for your specific drone. Set up the aircraft and make sure the latest firmware and software are installed. Familiarize yourself with the features, controls and screen/menu layouts of the control interface. Pick a web domain name and register it. Your website designer should be able to help you with this. Continue with logo and website design. Watch YouTube videos on maneuvers (see resources section for URLs).

Day 3: Stock Footage Site Registration. Research and choose reputable stock footage sites that accept drone footage and still images (see "resources" section for a list). Create an account on the platforms that do not require a portfolio to join. Look at what is popular and make a list of similar shots you can capture in your area. Continue website collaboration and logo work with designer throughout the next two weeks.

Day 4: Beginner Drone Maneuvers. These practice maneuvers will help you learn to control the drone to the point where it becomes second nature. It's a good idea to record your maneuvers and review the shots later because it's easier to be objective when you're not flying. For an online look at 15 basic flight maneuvers from The Pilot Institute, go to: https://www.youtube.com/watch?v=O0ydRf3 e5iM. Except where noted, make sure drone is connected to satellites for stability. **Maneuvers:** Launch/Hover/Precision Landing

Drone Skills: Master basic flight controls, stability, altitude & landing control.

Instructions

1. Hover the drone at eye level, maintaining a consistent altitude for 5 seconds without drifting off position. Change altitude and repeat until comfortable.

2. Practice hovering and maintaining stable flight at different altitudes. Notice how the light affects objects and scenes on the ground. Record video and take pictures to analyze later.

3. Precision Landing. With the aircraft in "Manual" mode, Practice landing the drone manually in a designated landing area. Switch to satellite mode and repeat. Enable Precision Landing to observe the drone's ability to land on its own.

Homework: Continue Web site Design and logo work

Days 5 & 6: Beginner Drone Maneuvers, continued. These maneuvers are best done in an area with lines such as an empty parking lot or a sports field. Start by marking the take-off spot and the end of your flight line with cones or some other marker.

Instructions

Maneuver 1: Basic Forward Flight. Start the drone and lift off to a height 4-5 feet above you.With the drone directly above the line and facing away from you, gently push the right control stick forward to move the drone forward and away. Maintain a constant speed and ensure the drone remains straight and level during the flight.

Maneuver 2: Backwards Flight Towards Pilot (From #1, above). At the end of the line, gently pull the right control stick back to move the drone backwards and towards you. You will be flying in reverse with the drone looking away from you. Come to a stop over the takeoff marker.

Maneuver 3: Forward Towards Pilot (From #2) Repeat #1 to the end of line marker. Once there, push the left control stick to the left or right to turn the aircraft until it faces you. Slowly push the right control stick forward and hold to fly the drone towards and facing you. Maintain a steady course and speed until you reach the take off point.

Homework: Review recorded footage at home and make notes. Explore Autonomous Flight. If your drone has auto flight functions, explore their use on the drone manufacturer's web site and in the handbook. These can include features such as **Point of Interest** (POI) where you circle an object or building, **TapFly** (DJI) which allows you to draw a flight path on the screen and automatically fly it, **ActiveTrack** (DJI) where your drone tracks a moving object, **Waypoint Navigation** for setting points that your drone will fly to and around, and **Hyperlapse** to take a moving time lapse video.

Day 7: Repeat basic maneuvers from day 6 and try your drone's auto flight functions. Sign up with "Aggregator" sites. Using the list from the "Resources" section, find and sign up with aggregator sites for freelance drone work. Take time to read other pilots' profiles & experience and model your profile after the successful ones.

Homework: Editing software & Website design. Download and install your choice of video editing software. Using the instructions in the "Resources" section of this book, find a YouTube or "LinkedIn Learning" video editing "Quick Start" course and follow it. Practice editing your drone footage into some kind of short video with music and basic titles. Finalize basic website design with splash page and contact/about pages.

Day 8: Beginner Drone Maneuvers, continued

Maneuver 1: Spot Landing. Choose a small landing spot and practice descending and landing the drone accurately within that area. Fly drone to small landing spot. Aim to land the drone on or within inches of a pre-marked spot. Repeat until comfortable.

Maneuver: Orbit. Drone Skills: Precision yaw and slide coordination while manually tracking a stationary object. This maneuver can be automated, but practicing it manually will hone your mastery of yaw and tracking skills.

Instructions: Select an object on the ground and push the left stick to the right slightly while simultaneously pushing the right stick to its right. Keep the object of interest in the monitor crosshairs by adjusting both stick movements slightly while flying. This is a good maneuver to record and playback later to see how you can improve in the future. Repeat maneuvers from previous days that you are unsure of.

Homework: Continue with editing lessons and practice.

Day 9: Intermediate Drone Maneuvers

Maneuver: Arc Flight. Simi-circle around a point. **Drone Skills:** Smooth flight and precise yaw control for cinematic shots.

Instructions: Find an empty baseball field and practice flying your drone in a sim-circle around the pitcher's mound while keeping the camera pointed at home plate. If possible, have an assistant stand at home plate while performing the maneuver and keep them in the cross hairs while moving from left to right. Launch and fly to an altitude of about eye level or higher. Starting at the left end of the simi-circle, push the left stick gently towards the right ("yaw") while simultaneously pushing the right stick slightly in the same direction. Keep home plate in the center of the shot. Slowly ease off on both sticks when reaching the end of the right arc. Repeat maneuver in the opposite direction.

Maneuver: Fly-throughs. **Drone Skills:** Improving precision and spatial awareness.

Instructions: Set up various obstacles or hoops and practice flying the drone through them one by one. Start by positioning yourself in front of the obstacles and flying towards them. Repeat the maneuver from a control position on the side of the obstacles so your POV is from the side while flying.

Maneuver: Circle (Various Versions). **Drone Skills:** Stick control

Instructions: Place a marker on the ground about 15 feet away from your launch point. Fly to a position about 10 feet from and facing the marker. Fly a tight circle around the marker without moving the camera. Repeat the maneuver while keeping the camera pointed at the marker and maintaining a consistent altitude and a steady shot.

Maneuver: Rectangle. **Drone Skills:** Stick and Camera Control

Instructions: Mark 4 points on the ground to form a rectangular flight area. With the camera pointed away from you at one corner, fly the drone in a rectangular pattern from marker to marker while maintaining a steady shot with the camera. Repeat with the camera pointed towards you.

Homework: Screen your work/Stock Footage Sites. Objectively analyze any shots you have recorded to this point. Make note of what you do well and what you need to improve. Add maneuvers to your next outing that target your shortcomings.

Go through stock footage sites and analyze the drone shots for movements and techniques. Make a list of what is popular and what you can emulate in your area (Iconic buildings, sites, beaches, scenics, etc).

Days 10, 11: Intermediate Maneuvers, Continued

Maneuver: Figure 8. **Drone Skills:** Stick control.

Instructions: Fly the camera in a figure 8 while keeping the camera facing in a consistent direction. Repeat by flying in the opposite direction. Repeat again flying backwards.

Maneuver: Slalom Course. **Drone Skills:** Obstacle navigation and precise control.

Instructions: Set up a slalom course with multiple obstacles and navigate through them without hitting any. Focus on maintaining speed and control through tight spaces. Repeat a number of times while increasing your constant speed on each attempt.

Homework: Continue with editing lessons and editing practice. Continue analyzing drone shots on stock footage sites. Plan a practice day to capture iconic and beauty shots that you have identified on stock footage sites as popular.

Day 12: Field trip to iconic and beauty sites identified previously. Using moves and techniques practiced in previous maneuvers, capture video and still shots with the aim of selling them to stock footage sites.

Days 13-15: Advanced Maneuvers for Cinematic Control. These maneuvers require more practice and flying time to develop your skills to the point where you don't think about what your fingers are doing. With enough practice, it's almost like your controller connected directly to your brain and the drone is being flown by your thoughts! To see many of these maneuvers demonstrated on video, follow the link in the "resources" section.

Maneuver: Smooth Ascend

Instructions: Identify a tall building that is safe to fly around. Frame the building so that only part of it is in the shot (for instance, the first floor and surrounding landscaping, sidewalk, etc). With the camera pointed slightly down (about 45 degrees), fly the drone straight up slowly so that your camera captures the building details. Stop at the top.

Maneuver: Pull out.

Instructions: Start at the ending of previous maneuver #1 above. Make sure the space behind your drone is clear. Put the building in the middle of the frame and point the camera straight at the building. Fly straight backwards slowly until the entire building is in the shot. Be sure to check your surroundings for obstacles before attempting this maneuver.

Maneuver: Partial Orbit (Wide Arc)

Instructions: Start from the end of previous maneuver #2 above. Pull back to a wide enough shot so that 3-4 buildings are in your shot with your main building in the center. Using the left stick to yaw (rotate) and the right stick to slide (left and right), very slowly fly in a simi-circle to the left keeping the main building centered. Repeat to the opposite direction. This is one of the most difficult moves to master smoothly with a drone, so practice it, record it, and watch it back to see how you can improve on it.

Maneuver: Push In (Fly in)

Instructions: Start at the end of previous maneuver #3 above. Fly in slowly until the building is tight in the frame. As your skill advances, use the gimbal to move the camera up or down slowly to change the position of the building in the shot. (Hint: know what your ending shot is before you start.)

Maneuver: Fly-in/descend while tilting camera up.

Instructions: This is one of the most difficult maneuvers to master smoothly due to the need to use three fingers: one on each of the control sticks and a third on the gimbal wheel. Find the gimbal control wheel and adjust it (in the settings) so that the gimbal speed and reaction time is reduced and comfortable for your style. Using the same building as in previous maneuvers, start with your drone extremely wide and higher than the subject building. Move the right stick forward to move the drone towards the subject and the left stick down so the drone is getting closer to the ground. At the same time, move the gimbal wheel to tilt the camera up slowly. Keep moving forward and descending until the top of the subject building breaks the horizon line.

Maneuver: Descend/tilt up and Ascend/tilt down. This is basically the same maneuver as #5 above except that you are much closer to the subject and you only fly up and down. The key is to match the camera movement speed with the flight speed so that the object of focus seems to be moving.

Instructions: Start with your drone above and close enough to the subject so that it fills the frame. Move the left stick down while simultaneously tilting the camera up with the gimbal wheel. Repeat the move in the opposite direction. Start at the bottom or middle of the building with the camera pointed up. Push the left stick up while tilting the camera down with the gimbal wheel.

Maneuver: Descend-reveal

Instructions: Start above and in front of your subject. Slowly pull the left stick towards you to make the drone descend and reveal the subject. You can also reverse the maneuver to reveal an object behind your first subject.

Maneuver: Manual object tracking. This maneuver can easily be done with the automated function of your drone (if available). However, practicing the shots manually will give you tremendous control over your aircraft and help you to master its movement to the point of it being second nature.

Instructions: (Follow) Fly the drone behind a moving subject, maintaining an optimal distance and adjusting camera tilt to capture dynamic chase shots. Version 2 (Lead): Fly in front of the subject leading them as you go.

Version 3 (Side Track): Fly beside the subject so that you are parallel with them as you track their movement.

Maneuver: Side Reveal

Instructions: Start with your drone behind an object that obscures your final subject. Slowly push the right control stick to the left or right to fly the drone sideways from behind the obstruction until your main subject is framed by the camera.

Version 2: Bottom Reveal. Start with your subject out of frame and the camera pointed straight ahead, but above it. Pull the left control stick down to descend, slowly bringing the subject into frame from the bottom.

Homework: Sort and upload your best shots to stock footage sites for sale.

At day 15, you should be able to control your drone well enough to capture video and still shots using beginner and some intermediate techniques. Continue practicing all the maneuvers with emphasis on those that are giving you trouble and don't forget to review your work with a critical eye. Remember, safety is paramount when practicing these maneuvers. Always fly in open areas away from people, buildings, and other obstacles. Happy flying and improving your skills!

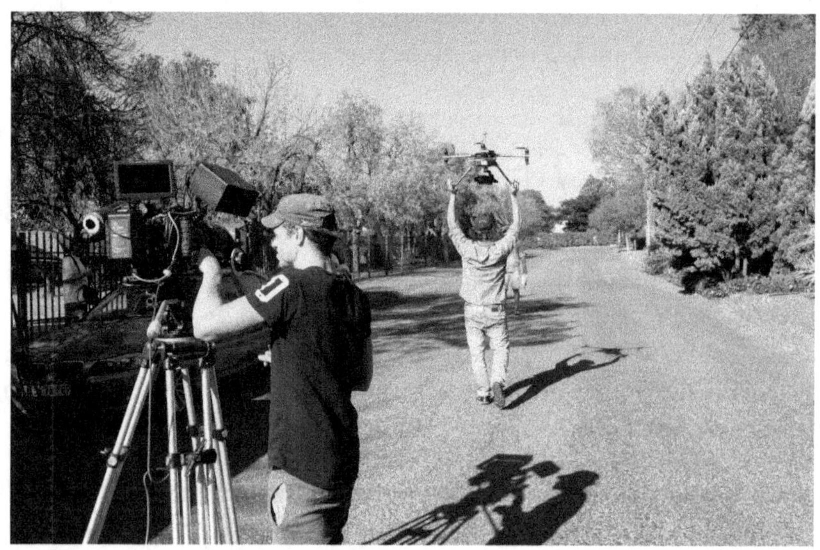

Practice makes perfect

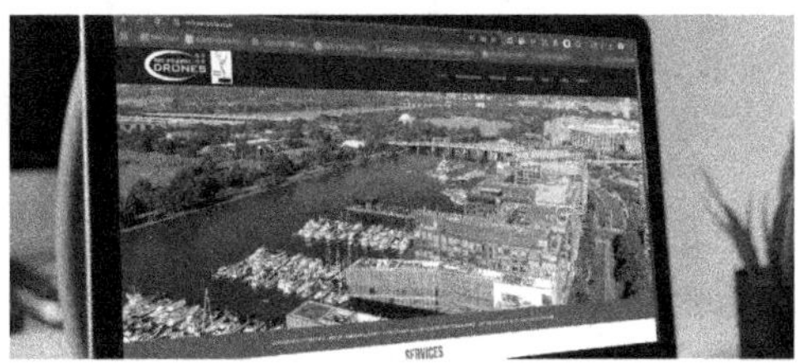

Your Free Gifts

For a 36-page guide with an extensive list of comprehensive resources including a **Free Part 107 Drone License Prep Course** (US-FAA), plus videos on flying, camera settings and shot examples, go to **www.MikeSobola.com/resources**, enter your email and I'll send you a link to the mini book full of additional material. I even include expanded information that gets "in the weeds" about aerial photography and video, camera settings, technical aspects of frame rate, size & capture, and more!

Go to **www.MikeSobola.com/resources** and enter your email to get your free access to these valuable resources. Here is a small sample:

A Short List of Additional Resources

Information on drone laws by country, state or city: https://drone-laws.com

U.S. Federal Aviation Administration Drone Information: https://www.faa.gov/uas

EU Drone License Information: https://www.easa.europa.eu/en/the-agency/faqs/drones-uas

Interactive FAA US Drone Airspace Map: https://faa.maps.arcgis.com/apps/webappviewer/index.html?id=9c2e4406710048e19806ebf6a06754ad

Free Drone Practice Maneuvers: https://dronedj.com/2020/07/16/drone-pilot-practice-exercises/

Wix.com Website Designer: Paule Doss: www.paulewebdesign.com.

Free Editing Platforms:

Filmora Wondershare Editing Platform: https://filmora.wondershare.net/

Canva: https://www.canva.com/video-editor/

CapCut: https://www.capcut.com

Clipchamp: https://clipchamp.com/en/

DaVinci Resolve: https://www.blackmagicdesign.com/products/davinciresolve

Moavi: https://www.movavi.com/video-editor-plus/

VideoProc Vlogger: https://www.videoproc.com/video-editing-software/

Free Music:

What is free music: https://www.silvermansound.com/understanding-music-licensing

Pixabay: https://pixabay.com/music/

Audionautix: https://audionautix.com/

Silverman Sound: https://www.silvermansound.com/understanding-music-licensing

Music For Makers: https://musicformakers.com/

This is just a sample. Please go to: **www.MikeSobola.com/resources** and enter your email for free access to an extensive bounty of the latest information including a FREE Part 107 course, demo and instructional videos, drone shot examples and more.

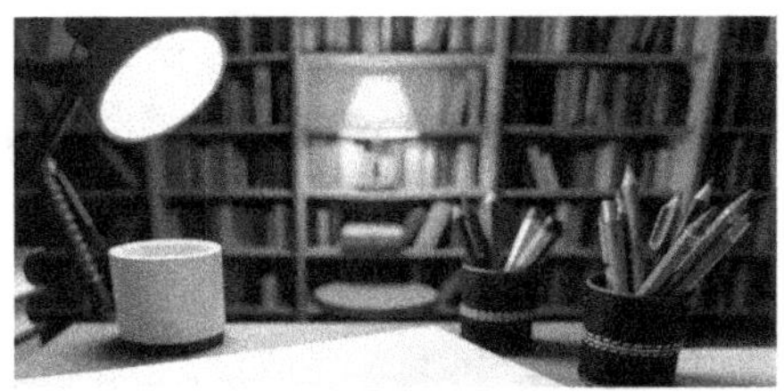

References

References are listed in alphabetical order.

Adam, & Adam. (2025, May 22). *Top 10 Drone-in-a-Box Solution in 2025.* XrTech Group. https://xrtechgroup.com/top-10-drone-in-a-box-solution/

Autonomous Drones In a Box | Dronehub – Digital transformation of your industry with autonomous drones in the box. (n.d.). https://dronehub.ai/

Chen, H., Lan Y., Fritz B.K., Hoffmann W.C. and Liu S. (2021). Review of agricultural spraying technologies for plant protection using unmanned aerial vehicle (UAV). Int. J. Agricult. Biolog. Engg., 14(1), 38-49.

Dengeru, Y., Ramasamy K., Allimuthu S., Balakrishnan S., Kumar A.P.M., Kannan B. and Karuppasami K.M. (2022). Study on Spray Deposition and Drift Characteristics of UAV Agricultural Sprayer for Application of Insecticide in Redgram Crop (Cajanus cajan L. Millsp.). Agronomy, 12(12), 3196.

Dock for X10. (n.d.). Skydio. https://www.skydio.com/dock

Drone inspection. (n.d.). https://enertrag.com/solutions-for-the-energy-transition/inspection-and-technical-operations/drone-inspection

DroneDeploy Dock Automation: Automated DJI Dock 2 integration for remote site monitoring. (n.d.). https://www.dronedeploy.com/product/dock-automation

DroneMatrix | Drone in the box. (n.d.). https://www.dronematrix.eu/

Farmonaut. (2025, September 28). *Best Agriculture Drone Sprayer 2025: Top Spray Drones.* Farmonaut®. https://farmonaut.com/precision-farming/best-agriculture-drone-sprayer-2025-top-spray-drones

Flanigan, M., & Flanigan, M. (2025a, February 28). *Agriculture drones in 2025: What's the future look like?* Avary Drone. https://avarydrone.com/blogs/learn/agriculture-drones-in-2025-whats-the-future-look-like

Flanigan, M., & Flanigan, M. (2025b, February 28). *Agriculture drones in 2025: What's the future look like?* Avary Drone. https://avarydrone.com/blogs/learn/agriculture-drones-in-2025-whats-the-future-look-like

Introduction to color spaces in video | Matrox Video. (n.d.). https://video.matrox.com/en/media/guides-articles/introduction-color-spaces-video

Jiang, Y., He, X., Song, J., Liu, Y., Wang, C., Li, T., Qi, P., Yu, C., & Chen, F. (2022). Comprehensive assessment of intelligent unmanned vehicle techniques in pesticide application: A case study in pear orchard. *Frontiers in Plant Science, 13*, 959429. https://doi.org/10.3389/fpls.2022.959429

Leading companies in agriculture drones market - DJI (China), Trimble Inc. (US), Parrot Drone SAS (France), Yamaha Motor Co., Ltd. (Japan) and AGEagle Aerial Systems Inc. (US). (n.d.-a). https://www.marketsandmarkets.com/ResearchInsight/agriculture-drones-market.asp

Leading companies in agriculture drones market - DJI (China), Trimble Inc. (US), Parrot Drone SAS (France), Yamaha Motor Co., Ltd. (Japan) and AGEagle Aerial Systems Inc. (US). (n.d.-b). https://www.marketsandmarkets.com/ResearchInsight/agriculture-drones-market.asp

Ltd, R. a. M. (n.d.-a). *Crop Spraying Drones Market Size, Share, Trends, Analysis, and Forecast 2025-2034 | Global Industry Growth, Competitive Landscape, Opportunities, and Challenges.* Research and Markets Ltd 2025. https://www.researchandmarkets.com/reports/6088013/crop-spraying-drones-market-size-share-trends

Ltd, R. a. M. (n.d.-b). *Crop Spraying Drones Market Size, Share, Trends, Analysis, and Forecast 2025-2034 | Global Industry Growth, Competitive Landscape, Opportunities, and Challenges.* Research and Markets Ltd 2025. https://www.researchandmarkets.com/reports/6088013/crop-spraying-drones-market-size-share-trends

Markets, R. A. (2025, October 15). Agri-Drones Industry Research Report 2025-2035: Market to Expand rapidly driven by strategic partnerships, startup innovation, and leading players including DJI, XAG, and Parrot drones. *GlobeNewswire*   *News*   *Room.*

https://www.globenewswire.com/news-release/2025/10/15/3167054/0/en/ Agri-Drones-Industry-Research-Report-2025-2035-Market-to-Expand-Rapi dly-Driven-by-Strategic-Partnerships-Startup-Innovation-and-Leading-Player s-Including-DJI-XAG-and-Parrot-Drones.html

McCullough, C. (2025, July 23). *US company introduces world's largest agricultural spray drone.* DirectIndustry e-Magazine. https://emag.directindustry.com/2024/09/18/us-company-introduces -worlds-largest-agricultural-spray-drone/

Medina, T. (2025, April 18). *Top 10 crop spraying drones of 2025: Reviews, comparisons, and buying guide.* DSLR-Pros. https://www.dslrpros.com/blogs/drone-trends/top-10-crop-spraying-d rones-of-2025-reviews-comparisons-and-buying-guide

Ombrulla. (n.d.). *AI Infrastructure Inspection | Drone inspection | Ombrulla.* Ombrulla. https://ombrulla.com/solutions/ai-infrastructure-inspection

Parkinson, C. (2023, June 12). *Percepto's drone-in-a-box solution - InDro Robotics.* InDro Robotics. https://indrorobotics.ca/perceptos-autonomous-dro ne-in-a-box/

Patented aerial drone in a box System NEST 250 | DronUS. (2022, May 26). Dronus. https://dronus.com/en/drone-in-a-box/

Percepto. (2023, June 14). *It's a new era in autonomous drones.* Percepto. http s://percepto.co/its-a-new-era-in-autonomous-drones/

Percepto Autonomous Solutions. (2023, December 13). *Autonomous site inspections guide - Percepto.* Percepto. https://percepto.co/autonomous-site-ins pections/

Percepto Autonomous Solutions. (2024a, September 13). *Remote Inspection & Monitoring of industrial Sites - PErCepTO.* Percepto. https://percepto.co/re mote-operations/

Percepto Autonomous Solutions. (2024b, December 4). *Autonomous inspection rounds with AIM - Percepto.* Percepto. https://percepto.co/inspection-rounds/

Research, S. (2019a). Unmanned Traffic Management Market Analysis | 2023-2028. In *stratviewresearch.com.* https://www.stratviewresearch.com/61 7/unmanned-traffic-management-market.html

Research, S. (2019b). Unmanned Traffic Management Market Analysis | 2023-2028. In *stratviewresearch.com*. https://www.stratviewresearch.com/617/unmanned-traffic-management-market.html

Saving 20% on Stack Inspections with the Elios 3. (n.d.). https://www.flyability.com/casestudies/stack-inspection

Shilin, W., Jianli S., Xiongkui H., Le S., Xiaonan W., Changling W., Zhichong W. and Yun L. (2017). Performances evaluation of four typical unmanned aerial vehicles used for pesticide application in China. Int. J. Agricult. Biolog. Engg., 10(4), 22-31

Shrivastava, A. (2025, May 5). 2025 Solar panel drone inspection costs: everything you need to know. *UAVSphere*. https://www.uavsphere.com/post/2025-solar-panel-drone-inspection-costs-everything-you-need-to-know

Team, V. (2025, September 12). Evolution of Asset Management: Traditional vs. software. *VLX*. https://vlx.ai/blog/the-evolution-of-asset-management-traditional-methods-vs-asset-inspection-software/

The Business Research Company. (2025). Crop Spraying Drones Global Market Report 2025. In *The Business Research Company*. https://www.thebusinessresearchcompany.com/report/crop-spraying-drones-global-market-report

The evolution history of agriculture drone sprayers-topxgunag.com. (n.d.). https://www.topxgunag.com/the-evolution-history-of-agriculture-drone-sprayers

The Ultimate ROI guide for infrared drone solar inspections – The Drone Life. (n.d.). https://thedronelifenj.com/the-ultimate-roi-guide-for-infrared-drone-solar-inspections/

Top 5 inspection software for drone building & construction. (n.d.). https://averroes.ai/blog/inspection-software-for-drone-building-and-construction

Wang, C., Liu Y., Zhang Z., Han L., Li Y., Zhang H., Wongsuk S., Li Y., Wu X. and He X. (2022). Spray performance evaluation of a six rotor unmanned aerial vehicle sprayer for pesticide application using an orchard operation mode in apple orchards. Pest Manage. Sci., 78(6), 2449-2466.

What is a LUT? (n.d.). https://lightillusion.com/what_are_luts.html

What's driving growth in the crop spraying drone market? (2024, February 5). Commercial UAV News. https://www.commercialuavnews.com/europe/what -s-driving-growth-in-the-crop-spraying-drone-market

Zhang, X. (n.d.). *Why Using AI is the future for Drone inspections.* https://info .qii.ai/blog/why-using-ai-is-the-future-for-drone-inspections

www.ingramcontent.com/pod-product-compliance
Lightning Source LLC
Chambersburg PA
CBHW071214130726
47998CB00002B/746